Climbing Knots

For Lefties and Righties

By Michael S. Noonan

Illustrations By
John McMullen and
Cathy Carlisle-McMullen

ICS BOOKS, Inc.

Merrillville, Indiana

ROCK!

Warning! Any type of climbing is dangerous and can result in serious injury or death. The material contained in this book is no substitute for qualified instruction, given under expert supervision.

This book is sold with no liability to the author, editors or publisher, expressed or implied, in the case of any and all damage, injury or death to the purchaser or reader.

CLIMBING KNOTS FOR LEFTIES AND RIGHTIES
BY MICHAEL S. NOONAN, ILLUSTRATED BY JOHN MCMULLEN
AND CATHY CARLISLE-MCMULLEN
Copyright © 1997 Michael Noonan
Illustrations © 1997 John McMullen and Cathy Carlisle-McMullen
10 9 8 7 6 5 4 3 2 1

Published by:
ICS Books, Inc.
1370 E. 86th Place
Merrillville, IN 46410
800-541-7323

Library of Congress Cataloging-in-Publication Data

Noonan, Michael Stewart, 1945-
    Climbing knots for lefties and righties / by Michael S. Noonan.
        p. cm.
    Includes bibliographical references and index.
    ISBN 1-57034-053-6 (pbk.)
    1. Climbing knots. I. Title.
    GV200.19.K56N66   1997   96-51757
    796.52'2—dc21   CIP

Contents

Introduction

Climbing! Seeking an oasis of freedom, whether it be a mountain summit or a cave within a cave. Whether it be in one's own back yard, in the woods by a gurgling stream, at a mountain timberline or on seashore crags.

Climbing provides almost limitless enjoyment, provided that climbers treat all of nature's wonders with respect, as a privilege for everyone to enjoy, including climbers who will follow in the future. With that privilege comes a responsibility to protect nature, the environment and fellow climbers.

Responsibility is both a cause and an effect. The development of climbing skills helps to reduce the possibility of damaging the environment. Listening and looking, reading and questioning; all help to develop and nurture a climber's skills. One result is that one learns to climb lightly, leaving only a minimal impact on the rock.

Responsibility is also an effect. Nature is unforgiving but very giving. An appreciation of the outdoors is a gift and one that grows with time. Appreciation also grows with experience, which comes partly from the refinement and polishing of skills.

One of the oldest climbing skills is knot tying. Successful knot tying is the result of proper rope and knot selection, practice and experience.

Proper rope selection has been simplified somewhat by recent technology. But there was climbing before kernmantle. The next section deals with ropes past and present, including material used, both natural and man-made.

Proper knot selection involves more than a simple book. This book includes the repertory of knots which are actually in use and chosen by climbers; some knots which were used in the past are not included, as they were discarded as ineffectual or dangerous in the evolution of climbing knots and techniques.

This is not a book on the various types of climbing (e.g., bouldering, rock climbing, mountaineering, caving, etc.) nor is it a book on the various techniques of climbing (e.g., face climbing, prusiking, rappelling, double roping, etc.). It is assumed that the reader already has a basic knowledge of or background in one or more of the various forms of the sport of climbing, including techniques and equipment. A short synopsis of each discipline will be given in the introduction of the respective chapter.

This is a book about proper knot selection. However, there are trade-offs, so there may not be a perfect knot for a particular application. Experience derived from practice and proper climbing instruction will help narrow down the search for and selection of the optimum knot.

A description of the various types of ropes is given in the next section. Then there is a section dealing with the several criteria, requirements and trade-offs involved when choosing the optimum knot for a particular application. The chapter concludes with several definitions concerning ropes and knots, and the procedures and conventions which are used in the book to integrate and simplify the text description and the knot construction illustrations. Included as examples are the several safety knots, i.e., knots which are used to secure the free ends of a climbing knot after dressing, setting and tightening the particular climbing knot. After being tied, all climbing knots should have their free ends secured to further help provide added reliability and safety.

Subsequent chapters deal with knots used in anchoring and belaying, prusiking and rappelling, and hauling. The final chapter contains knots which have not been previously mentioned and which are used around the base camp.

1

Climbing, Ropes
and Knots

Ropes

The first ropes to be used were simple vines which occur naturally in woods and forests. They're still used around the world.

To make stronger and more reliable ropes, man began to fashion them with natural fibers, such as cotton, hemp, jute, flax (linen), manila, sisal and coconut fiber. Also used were papyrus, leather or hide, horsehair and human hair.

Metal wire resulted in strong ropes for certain applications. Early metals used included copper, bronze, nickel, etc. Many more alloys are now available for rope construction.

Recent developments include synthetic filaments, such as nylon, Dacron, polypropylene, polyethylene, Kevlar and glass fibers.

Whether natural or man-made, both types of rope have a common thread: the vegetable or animal fiber, the synthetic filament and the wire.

The fiber (natural or synthetic) is the building block used in making ropes.

Take two equal length fibers and lay them side-by-side. Hold the two fibers together at one end with the thumb and forefinger of the left hand; with the thumb and forefinger of the right hand grasp the two fibers near the left hand and rotate the two fibers simultaneously around each other in a clockwise manner. The process is called twisting. More specifically, right-handed twisting.

A yarn consists of two or more fibers twisted (i.e., spun) together. In ropemaking, a thread is the same as a yarn (sewing thread consists of two, three or more yarns twisted together).

A strand consists of two or more yarns twisted (i.e., formed) together and is generally left-handed.

A rope consists of three or more strands (left-handed) twisted together (i.e., laid) and is right-handed. It's also called plain-laid rope. A hawser is a large plain-laid rope with a circumference of over five inches.

To summarize, a right-handed rope consists of three or more left-handed strands, each of which is formed with two or more right-handed yarns. There are several reasons for making the alternating-hand twists: the opposing twists increase the friction between the fibers, yarns and strands, thus increasing the overall strength of the rope; they also make the rope more dense and compact, thus reducing moisture absorption; they also give the rope more stability, i.e., lessen the tendency to unravel.

A cable consists of three plain-laid ropes twisted (or laid up) together (i.e., closed) and is left-handed.

To tell the lay of a rope hold it vertically. The strands of a right-handed (or right-laid) rope go upward from left-to-right.

Similarly, for a left handed rope, the strands go upward from right-to-left.

Figure 1–1 Right-handed Rope   **Figure 1–2 Left-handed Rope**

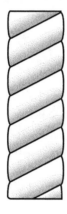
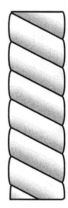

Under load or stress, a rope will twist and try to rotate. A right-handed rope is often used side-by-side with a left-handed rope, e.g., fishing seines and nets; the opposite twists compensate each other so the seine has less tendency to roll up.

When four strands are plain-laid, there remains a hole in the center. When the center space is filled in with a smaller rope (called the heart), the entire assembly is known as a four-strand rope or a shroud-laid rope.

Backhanded rope, also known as reverse-laid rope, is a right-handed rope which is composed of three or four right-handed strands, which are made up with right-handed yarns. It's more flexible than plain-laid rope but is more subject to abrasion and wear, is difficult to splice and absorbs moisture readily.

The six-strand rope is a right-handed rope with a heart; it's stiff, has high abrasion resistance but is less strong than a three- or four-strand rope.

In addition to twisted ropes, there are braided ropes and double-braided ropes (with a braided core covered by a woven sleeve, or sheath). Static kernmantle rope consists of a core of parallel fibers (a bundle) covered by a woven sleeve. A dynamic kernmantle rope consists of a core of parallel strands (each composed of twisted fibers) covered by a woven sleeve.

Included for completeness are the following types of lines:

- A shock cord, which consists of a bundle of parallel rubber strands covered by a woven sleeve.
- Webbing is a band of material which is woven of nylon or Dacron (also cotton, hemp or jute) and is very strong. It is flat and is either a single band or a double band (hollow flat, or tubular).
- Monofilament, made of nylon.

Factors involved in rope selection include the following:

The strength of a rope is very important. Breaking strength is a static parameter; pull on the rope until it breaks. The safe working load is a percentage of the breaking strength; for a new rope, it's about 25% of the breaking strength and decreases as the rope sustains average use (mountain climbers consider it about 10% or less).

Elasticity is a measure of how much a rope stretches. Medium elasticity means that the rope provides a shock absorber effect.

A rope must have sufficient abrasion resistance to nicks, cuts and chafing.

The dynamic strength of a rope is determined by the breaking strength, elasticity and abrasion resistance of the rope. It includes both the strength needed to survive a direct impact (e.g., a fall) and the strength required to survive a lateral shock to the rope which is wound through a pulley, suspended over the edge of a cliff, etc., where a high resistance to cuts, abrasion and fiber deformation is of paramount importance.

A rope should be easy to handle. A soft-laid rope, with few twists per inch of rope, handles easily, doesn't tend to kink and is stronger than a hard-laid rope, although a hard-laid rope has better abrasion resistance.

A rope should be as light as possible, with a diameter which is suited to the particular application.

It should have low water absorption. A wet or saturated rope is heavier and sometimes weaker than when dry.

High visibility is sometimes desirable and often available with some types of rope, notably the synthetics.

Some ropes are prone to damage from heat, sunlight and certain chemicals. They must be protected from harmful agents and properly stored when not in use.

Spliceability is a factor when choosing natural and wire ropes.

Knotability is an important consideration when selecting a rope. When a knot is tied in a rope, or made to connect two ropes, the operating criteria of the rope are degraded, in general. Most knots weaken a rope. If a knot is made in a limp rope, there is a possibility of the knot's slipping, capsizing, spilling and collapsing. If the rope has too much stretch, it is difficult to properly tighten and correctly seat the knot, thus reducing its strength; also, after even a short period of non-use, the rope will try to resume its non-stretched length and the knot will have to be re-tightened to prevent its slipping. A knot tied in a rope which absorbs moisture will also lose strength when the moisture evaporates.

However, knots have been designed and developed to take into account all of the above constraints, although not all at the same time. A judicious or experienced choice from a selection of special-purpose knots (also sometimes one of the general-purpose knots) will result in an optimum, strong and secure, reliable yet simple-to-tie knot. More will follow in the upcoming section on knot criteria and selection.

Natural Fiber Ropes

The following ropes are available, some of which are sill in wide usage:

Hemp is a fiber (soft if harvested at pollination, strong and coarse at maturity) which comes from a tall herb (three to fifteen feet high, depending on climate and soil type), Cannabis sativa, which is native to Asia but is now also naturalized or cultivated in many parts of the world. Most hemp ropes are tarred (to prevent rotting) and are used in a wide variety of applications, mainly under static load; however, it has been largely replaced by wire rope.

Manila is a fiber obtained from leafstalks of abaca, Musa textilis, an herb of the banana family. It's native to the Philippines and is cultivated to a lesser extent in Central America. Outer, course fibers are cultivated at maturity and range from six to ten feet in length (inner, finer fibers are fifteen feet long and are used for weaving cloth). Manila rope doesn't need tarring and is used in applications which require strength, ease of handling and safety (e.g., climbing, mooring, etc.).

Sisal is a fiber obtained from the leaves of an arid-environment plant, Agave sisalana, a member of the lily family. It's native to the West Indies and is now grown in Mexico and other tropical countries. Fibers are up to five feet in length. It's about half as strong as manila and doesn't stand wetting well; however, when mixed with hemp it is used for towing and mooring.

Linen is a fiber obtained from the stems of the flax plant, Linum usitatissimum. Flax is primarily a temperate-region plant and ranges in height from twelve to forty inches; the taller varieties are sparsely branched and used for fiber production (the seed producing varieties have shorter stems and are more heavily branched; they are cultivated for their seed, from which is extracted linseed oil). Linen ropes are about twice as strong as manila ropes.

Jute is a fiber obtained from the stems of the woody herb, Corchorus capsularis, a member of the linden family. The plants grow as tall as fourteen feet and are cultivated in tropical countries throughout the world, but most jute is grown in alluvial soils of river valleys in India. The fibers are yellowish-white, soft and lustrous and are used in the manufacture of rope, twine and other cordage, and also of burlap and gunny.

Cotton is a fiber obtained from the flower buds of small trees and shrubs of the genus Gossypium, a member of the mallow family. The fiber is a seed hair, i.e., a thin flattened tubular cell with a pronounced spiral twist, which is attached to a seed. Individual fibers are from a half inch to two and a half inches long. Cotton is white, soft and used to make yarn, cloth and cordage which is easy to handle and normally braided.

Coir is a fiber obtained from the outer husk of a coconut, which is the fruit of the tree, Cocis nucifera, of the palm family. Cultivation is widely distributed throughout the tropical regions of the world. The fibers are used to make matting and ropes. Coir is coarse, reddish in color and is not very strong. But it floats. It's used as a heaving line to connect to and lead other ropes to a mooring. It's also spliced into wire or manila ropes to give them greater spring. And when towed behind a vessel, it calms the sea somewhat by floating on it.

Synthetic Ropes

Compared to natural fiber ropes, synthetic ropes are stronger for their size, lighter, easier to handle and work, don't swell when wet, don't rot or mildew and run more easily through pulleys and chocks. Due to lower abrasion resistance, synthetic ropes are mostly braided or double-braided; construction techniques include both increasing the number of times per inch that the yarn bundles cross, and the tightness of the bundles. All ropes, whether natural, synthetic or wire, should be protected from chafing and wear.

Synthetic fibers, or filaments, include the following:

Nylon a polyamide fiber, is more than twice as strong as manila or linen and has an elasticity of 20 to 25%. It is 10 to 15% weaker when wet, but even then it is still stronger than other synthetics and retains its elasticity, unlike others which lose elasticity when wet. When double-braided rope is abraded, it forms a protective fuzzy surface which helps to reduce further abrasion. Nylon ropes can be substantially weakened by acids and oils, and when not in use should be kept out of the sunlight. Nylon ropes tie and untie easily and are used extensively in climbing and caving.

Kevlar, another polyamide, is a high-temperature-resistant fiber which is very strong. Kevlar rope has near zero stretch but is subject to both internal and external abrasion. It has low dynamic longitudinal energy absorption ability and breaks easily when knotted, although it does have some uses as a lightweight substitute for steel cable. Kevlar has high latitudinal energy absorption ability and is used for bulletproof vests.

Dacron a polyester fiber, retains most of its breaking strength when wet. It is about 75% as strong as nylon, has very little stretch and has good resistance to most acids and alkalis. Dacron ropes are used mainly in static applications.

Polyethylene, a polyolefin fiber, is not quite twice as strong as manila. It has little stretch, high resistance to acid and a low melting point. A polyethylene rope has positive floatation and is used as a tow rope in water skiing and in rescue work, even though it has a tendency to kink and snarl.

Polypropylene is another polyolefin fiber. A rope made with it is stronger than with polyethylene and more resistant to heat and friction. It's less resistant to sunlight. It also has positive floatation and is used as a tow rope in water skiing and in rescue work.

Glass fibers are made from silica (derived from sand, flint or quartz) which is fused at high temperatures with borates or phosphates. Continuous multifilament yarns may be braided into ropes which are strong, chemically stable and resistant to fire and water.

Wire Ropes

Wire is an elongated, flexible filament made of ductile metal and produced in various diameters. Metals most often used in rope making include steel, iron, copper and bronze. Wire ropes have high tensile strength and abrasion resistance and a wide range of flexibility, which depends on the number or wires in each strand (the more wires in a strand, the more flexible the rope).

Most wire ropes consist of wires laid or twisted into strands, then strands laid together to form the rope. For high density and maximum friction, geometry constrains the numbers of wires laid into strands; standard numbers include 1, 7, 12, 19, 24, 37 and even 61 wires for the most flexible rope (it consists of 6 strands of 61 wires each and is known as a 6 by 61 rope). Most ropes consist of 1 strand (e.g., a 1 by 19 rope, in which the wires are of two or three different diameters), 6 strands or 7 strands (e.g., a 7 by 7 rope).

In a standard rope, the strands are left-laid and the rope is right-laid.

In a long-laid rope, both the strands and the rope are of the same lay. It's more flexible and has higher abrasion resistance than standard rope.

Some ropes are laid around a heart, if there would otherwise remain a space in the center of the rope.

Knots and Knotting

A rope is a tool. When knots and loops are tied in the rope, it becomes a machine, transferring power from a source of energy to a load.

A rope is subjected to three forces: a longitudinal force called pull, directed axially down the length of the rope; a torsional, or rotational, force which produces twist; and a latitudinal force called resistance (e.g., a guard rope at the edge of a cliff). When knots are tied in the rope, it is also subjected to frictional forces.

The optimum knot for a task, which often involves trade-offs, is a result of both proper selection and proper tying. Proper selection comes from experience, or by taking advice from someone who has experience. Proper tying results in balancing and optimizing pull, twist, resistance and friction and comes from skill, developed by experiment and practice.

Criteria which are involved in and influence knot selection include the following:

Simplicity is very important. Most strong knots are simple to tie. A knot may have to be tied while under load or strain, or it may have to be tied quickly before an anticipated load is applied. A complex knot may be stronger but a knot which is easy to remember is easy to tie. Mountain climbers and rappellers need to know how to tie several knots with one hand (only one at a time, of course).

The strength of the knot is dependent on not only the strength of the rope but also on the knot selected. Choose the knot which has few sharp turns in order to minimize fiber deformation, compression and breakage.

Security and reliability are also very important. A properly chosen and tied knot will hold, whether it is constantly under load or alternating between strain and relaxation. The properly chosen knot depends on the material of which the rope is made, different materials or diameters if two ropes are being connected together, and sometimes depends on the surface of an object to which the rope is to be secured, e.g., a rope hitched to a smooth pole or to a rough post. Proper dressing and setting (i.e., tightening all parts) of a knot is required for security; sometimes gloves, pliers and body weight are needed to properly seat the knot. Knots should be tightened in one steady motion, rather than in stages. Then pull it again to see if it breaks or spills. Better then than when it's needed.

Some applications require a knot which can be easily readjusted without the need to untie and re-tie it, e.g., a middle climber loop adjustment.

Other applications require a knot which can be untied easily and quickly, e.g., escaping a belay to help a fallen climber.

Knots should be tied in the comfort of one's home, if and when possible. Or at base camp. Rather than trying to throw a rig as the sun is quickly going down. In the cold. While sneezing with tearing eyes and a runny nose. Alone. And watching a squall line approaching.

A piece of rope has two ends. The end in which the knot, bend or hitch is made is called the working end; it's also known as the free end, running end, bitter end, tag end, and the fall of the rope.

The stationary part of the rope not involved in knotting is called the standing part or the hauling part of the rope.

When a knot is made in the bight (e.g., Bowline on a Bight), neither end of the rope is used in the construction, only a section of the rope which is between the ends.

When two ropes are connected together, they are bent together, e.g., the Overhand Bend.

When a rope is secured to an object, it is bent or hitched to the object, which could include the rope itself.

In the illustrations to follow, when two ropes are bent (tied) together, the diameter of one is drawn larger than the other (i.e., both a large-point pen and a fine-point pen are used), done for clarity and to simplify the visual process of tying the knot. When two ropes are of different diameters, the text will state so.

Many knots have more than one name; the same knot is used in different applications and is named differently by the climber, caver, camper, sailor, fisherman, farmer, etc. The most common name will be capitalized.

Security Knots

As previously mentioned in the introduction, all climbing knots should have their free ends secured. It helps prevent the knot from loosening and provides added reliability and safety.

The simplest safety backup knot is the Overhand Knot, shown (Figure 1–3) securing a free end of a climbing knot; the top is the standing part of the climbing knot and the bottom line is the free end.

Figure 1–3 Overhand Knot
Right

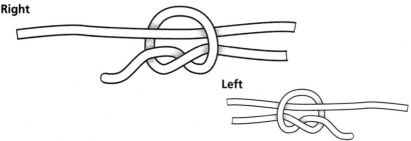

Left

Two Half Hitches (Figure 1–4) are used to secure the loose ends of other knots for greater security; in addition, it is a stand-alone knot, used to attach a rope to a post, ring or to another rope.

Figure 1–4 Two Half Hitches
Right

The One-Sided Grapevine Knot (Figure 1–5), also known as the Half-Double Fisherman's Knot, is also used to secure the free end of a climbing knot.

Figure 1–5 One-Sided Grapevine Knot

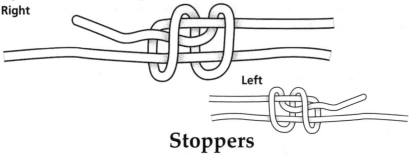

Stoppers

To keep from rappelling off the end of a rope or to keep the end of a line from being pulled through a pulley, hole or part of another knot, one can use a Figure Eight Knot (Figure 1–6).

Figure 1–6 Figure Eight Knot

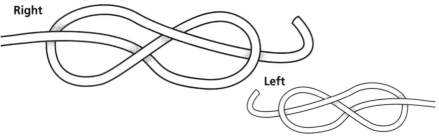

Some climbers prefer a Stevedore's Knot (Figure 1–7), also known as a Figure Nine Knot.

Figure 1–7 Stevedore's Knot

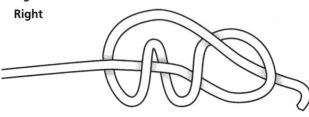

To lock off a belay plate, many climbers use an Overhand Loop (Figure 1–8).

Figure 1–8 Overhand Loop

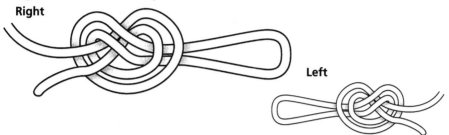

A carabiner (Figure 1–9) can be used to lock off a knot. An example is shown, using a double line Buntline Hitch (also known as an Inside Clove Hitch and as Studding-Sail Tack Bend).

Figure 1–9 Carabiner Stopper

Right

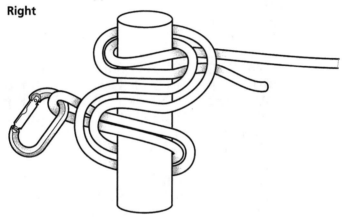

2

Anchor Knots

Introduction
Anchor Loops
   Bowline
   Mountaineering Bowline
   FIGURE EIGHT LOOP (Figure Eight on a
     Bight, Guide Knot)
Anchor Slings
   Endless Loop
   Runner
   Girth Hitch
   GRAPEVINE KNOT (Double Fisherman's Knot)
   BARREL KNOT (Triple Fisherman's Knot)
   OVERHAND BEND (Ring Bend, Tape Knot)
   FIGURE EIGHT BEND (Flemish Bend)
   Overhand Loop
Self-Equalizing Anchors
   French Bowline
   Portuguese Bowline
   Bowline on a Bight
   THREE LOOP BOWLINE (Triple Bowline)
Opposition Anchors
Backup Anchors
   Sling
   Interconnected Figure Eight Loops
   Interconnected Bowlines
   French Bowline
Nooses
   Slip Knot
   Figure Eight Noose
   Running Bowline

Introduction

An anchor should be as strong as the climbing rope, stable and nondirectional. A natural anchor (e.g., a tree) should be used whenever possible. When using an artificial anchor (a chock, cam device, etc.), test it with bodyweight before using it; two or more placements may be needed to make it strong enough and nondirectional.

An anchor should be backed up by another anchor when possible. Also, two slings, when used, are normally better than one, when there is room for both.

Anchor Loops

To conserve equipment and time, natural anchors should be used whenever possible.

Also, minimize the number of knots in a rigging whenever possible, as any knot binds and twists the rope and lessens the breaking strength of a rope. Use friction and gravity to advantage; the simple anchor shown (Figure 2–1) saves a rope pad and a possible deviation if the lip edge is sharp or rough.

Figure 2–1 Natural Anchors

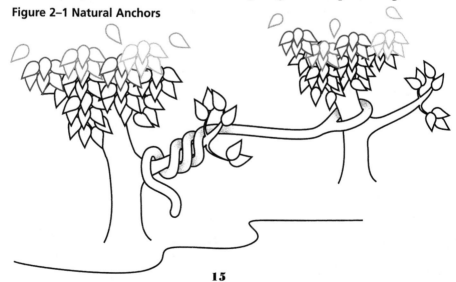

Several turns around an object (e.g., a tree) provides a large amount of friction. A rope pad or burlap sack around the tree limb (or trunk) helps to lessen rope abrasion and is recommended. The loop knot can be untied while under tension and a climber or load can be raised or lowered if need be.

Three knots often used to make a loop around the tree in the above illustration are the Bowline, the Mountaineering Bowline and the Figure Eight Loop.

The Bowline (Figure 2–2), if properly made, will not slip or jam. It's easy to tie and untie, even after heavy and repeated loading. The free end should be secured by an Overhead Knot (not shown).

Figure 2–2a Bowline
Right

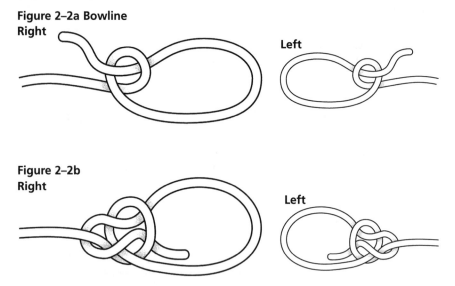

Left

Figure 2–2b
Right

Left

The Bowline is also looped through a swami belt or harness to secure a lead climber or belayer. It's also used to secure a foot loop to a Prusik Knot, Ascender Knot, etc.

The Mountaineering Bowline (Figure 2–3) is stronger and more secure than the Bowline and is also easy to tie and untie after loading. Make two eye loops instead of one eye loop as in the Bowline. Secure the free end with an Overhand Knot.

Figure 2–3a Mountaineering Bowline
Right

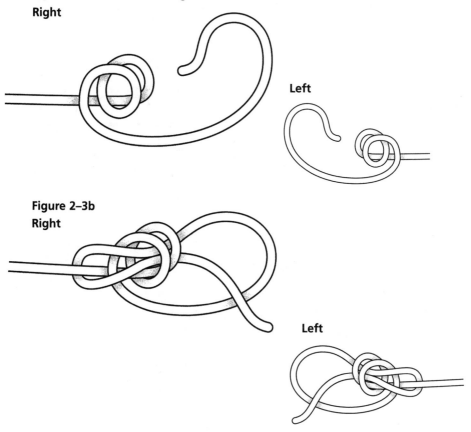

Left

Figure 2–3b
Right

Left

The Figure Eight Loop (Figure 2–4), also known as a Figure Eight on a Bight or a Guide Knot, is used to secure anchors, climbers and belayers. When the loop can't be simply slipped over an anchor, first tie a Figure Eight Knot in the line and then lead the free end around (or through) the anchor and back through the knot.

**Figure 2–4a Figure Eight Loop
Right**

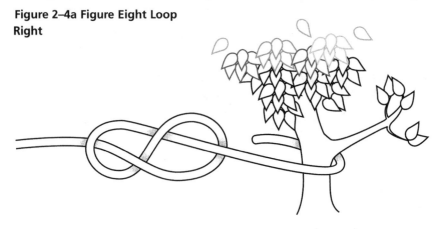

**Figure 2–4b
Right**

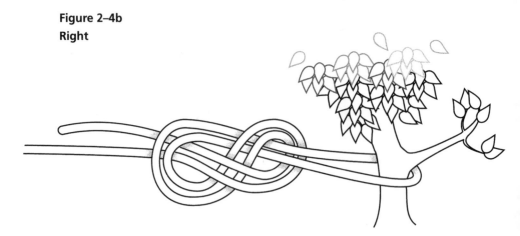

If the loop can be slipped over an anchor, one can simply tie it in the bight.

The knot is also used to secure end climbers and belayers and is used by some climbers as a middleman's knot when tied in the bight.

Anchor Slings

An anchor sling is an endless loop which connects an anchor to a belayer or climber. A runner is a sling which connects an anchor to a carabiner, through which the climbing rope passes but is not secured; runners are used when the lead climber places protection on a climb and they are also used to construct deviations which lead the climbing rope away from sharp edges, abrasive walls, waterfalls, etc.

An anchor sling (and runner) which has been and continues to be used is one which is girth hitched around the anchor (Figure 2–5).

Figure 2–5 Girth Hitch

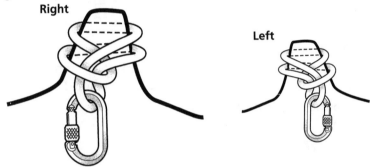

If a single rope is used to make the sling, connect the free ends with a Grapevine Knot (Figure 2–6), also known as a Double Fisherman's Knot.

Figure 2–6 Grapevine Knot

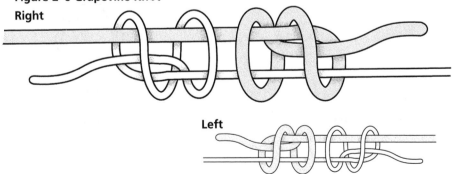

When setting the knot, use body weight and pliers to tighten it, as the free ends can be pulled into the knot by a sudden pull or impact on the line. Place the sling so that the knot can't rub against anything.

Some climbers prefer the Barrel Knot (Figure 2–7), also call the Triple Fisherman's Knot.

Figure 2–7 Barrel Knot

Right

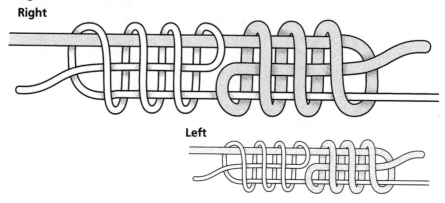

Left

It's very strong, but very difficult to untie.

Rather than girth hitching an anchor sling (or runner), many climbers prefer to double the loop around the anchor (Figure 2–8).

Figure 2–8 Double-Looped Anchor Sling

Right

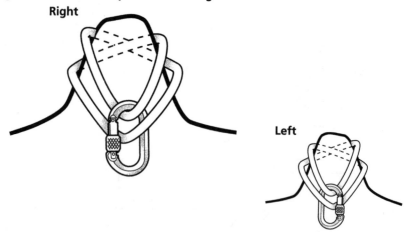

Left

Two identical slings could also be looped around the anchor.

When using webbing (one inch preferred), double the loops and tie the free ends with an Overhand Bend (Figure 2–9), also called the Ring Bend, Tape Knot and Water Knot; tie an Overhand Knot in one of the ends, then lead the other end back through the knot, set and tighten.

Figure 2–9 Overhand Bend

Right

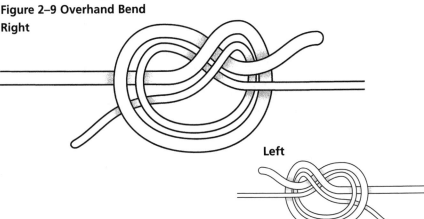

Left

Some climbers prefer the Figure Eight Bend (Figure 2–10), also called Flemish Bend. It's easier to untie than the Overhand Bend.

Figure 2–10 Figure Eight Bend

Right

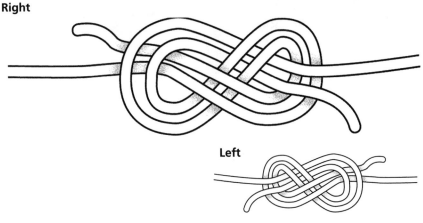

Left

To lessen the chance of an anchor sling or runner being pulled off the anchor, tie an Overhand Loop (Figure 2–11) in the webbing and tighten the loop around the anchor.

Figure 2–11 Overhand Loop
Right

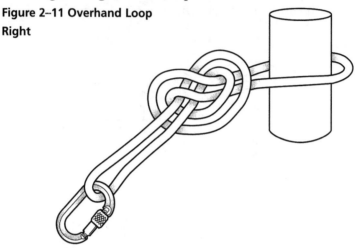

Most climbers use doubled slings and runners. In the preceding application, one can either double the line to make the sling, or use two identical slings, or one can rig two separate but nearby anchors (Figure 2–12).

Figure 2–12 Two-Sling Anchor
Right

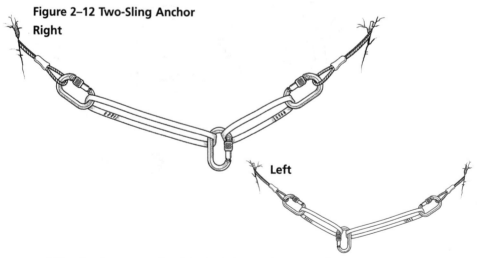

Left

If both slings are doubled, failure of one anchor need not result in failure of the second anchor.

If the preceding anchor rig isn't nondirectional with the available slings, rig the two anchors using a single sling with an Overhand Knot tied in the sling at a point which will lead in the direction of a fall when under tension (Figure 2–13). Secure the carabiner through both loops to keep it from sliding when under load.

Figure 2–13 Single Sling with Overhand Knot

Right

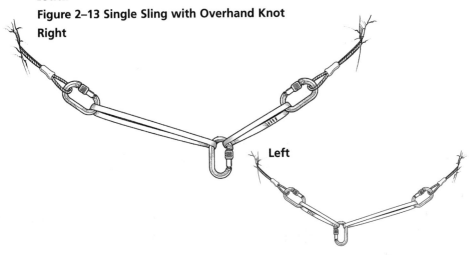

Left

Self-Equalizing Anchors

A French Bowline (Figure 2–14) is used by some climbers to rig two anchors to a climbing rope.

Figure 2–14 French Bowline

Right

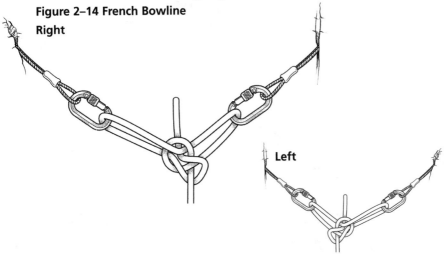

Left

With two added carabiners, the two loops can be rigged to three anchors (Figure 2–15).

Figure 2–15 Three-Anchor Rig
Right

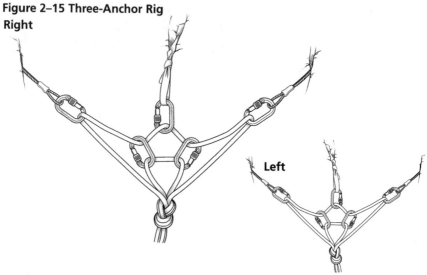

The two loop Portuguese Bowline and Bowline on a Bight can also be rigged as self-equalizing anchors, with two or three anchors.

The Portuguese Bowline is shown(Figure 2–16):

Figure 2–16a Portuguese Bowline
Right

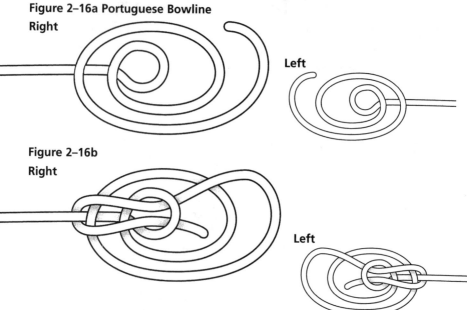

Less easy to adjust than the French and Portuguese Bowlines, the Bowline on a Bight is illustrated (Figure 2–17):

Figure 2–17a Bowline on a Bight
Right

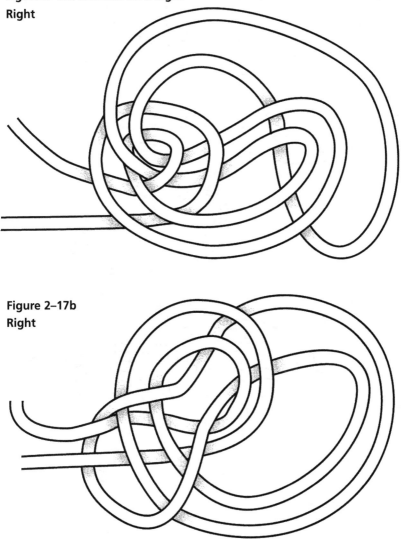

Figure 2–17b
Right

All three two-loop bowlines have also been used in rescue work, in which one loop is used as a seat sling and the second as a chest cling. Also the Bowline on a Bight is used as a mainline knot, both by end and middle climbers.

Three anchors can be directly connected to a Three Loop Bowline (Figure 2–18), sometimes called a Triple Bowline.

Figure 2–18a Three Loop Bowline
Right

Left

Figure 2–18b
Right

Left

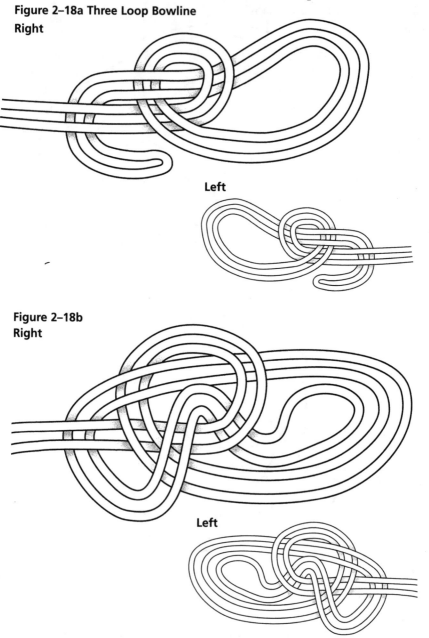

Members of the bandoliers of 'biners brigade use a long sling (perhaps doubled), six carabiners and a single loop to rig three anchors; (Figure 2–19) one of the 'biners is clipped inside the sling loop as a precaution in case any two of the three anchors fail. The single loop in the climbing rope is made with a Bowline, Figure Eight Loop or some other climber's favorite.

Figure 2–19 Three-Anchor Rig with Sling

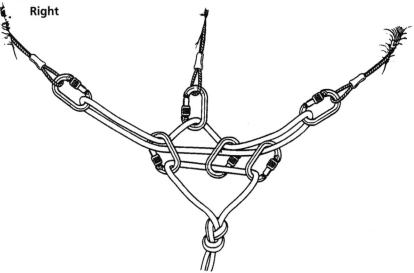

Right

Opposition Anchors

The previous anchors and anchor placements are or are rigged to be nondirectional. In addition, multiple anchor points supplement each other, each being able to withstand a fall from a failure of a top or bottom placement or runner.

There are also circumstances when two anchors or anchor placements are rigged to complement each other, e.g., to rig a deviation, chocks or nuts in a horizontal crack, etc. The two anchor points are rigged in opposition, in which the opposition can make one or two marginal placements (e.g., a placement which is directional or cannot stand alone, or both) solid and nondirectional.

Several methods are illustrated (Figure 2–20). Some placements require constant tension while other don't. Some require the use of both a long and a short sling.

Figure 2–20a Complementary Anchors

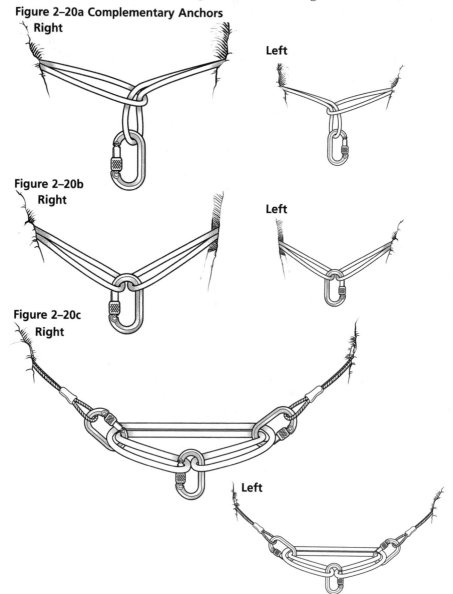

Backup Anchors

In addition to the primary anchor, which may have from one to several placements in the rig, there may be a need for a backup anchor.

Use natural anchors whenever possible. Three methods of rigging a backup anchor are illustrated, using a sling, a single line pair of Figure Eight Loops and a pair of interconnected Bowlines.

When using a sling to rig a backup anchor (Figure 2–21), loop the climbing rope both around the primary anchor and through the sling. Adjust the sling to remove any slack between the anchors.

Figure 2–21 Backup Anchor with Sling

If both anchors have carabiners or can be lassoed, a single line pair of Figure Eight Loops can be rigged (Figure 2–22) by first tying the backup loop in the bight and securing it to the backup anchor and then tying the primary loop in the bight and securing it. If neither anchor can be lassoed (e.g., two trees) and neither loop can be tied in the bight, first tie the primary loop loosely, with enough rope in the free end (which becomes the standing part in the backup loop) to make the backup loop (you'll soon see why, especially with a 600 foot climbing rope).

Figure 2–22 Backup Anchor with Figure Eight Loops

Make the backup loop, tighten it and then remove any slack between the anchors and tighten the primary loop.

When rigging a pair of interconnected Bowlines (Figure 2–23), first loosely tie the primary loop, leaving enough free end to tie the backup loop.

Figure 2–23 Backup Anchor with Bowlines

Make the backup loop, tighten it and then remove any slack between the anchors and tighten the primary loop.

Some climbers prefer to use a French Bowline, using one loop each for the two anchors.

Nooses

Some climbers prefer a constricting noose for securing a climbing rope to a certain anchor (e.g., a tree).

The simplest is the Slip Knot (Figure 2–24), also called an Overhand Noose, Running Knot, Running Overhand and Slip Noose. The free end should be secured after the loop has been tightened.

Figure 2–24 Slip Knot
Right

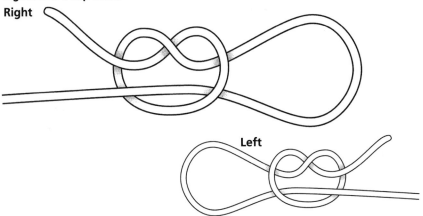

Left

The Figure Eight Noose (Figure 2–25) also has several other names, e.g., Figure Eight Running Knot, Grocer's Hitch, Packer's Knot and Stationer's Knot.

Figure 2–25 Figure Eight Noose
Right

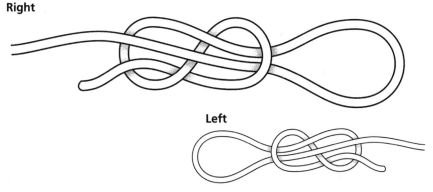

Left

A noose may also be made by leading a bight made in the standing part through a loop already made, e.g., the Running Bowline (Figure 2–26).

Figure 2–26 Running Bowline

Right

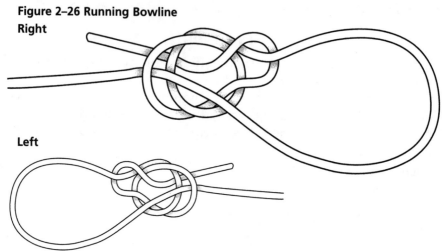

Left

3

Belays

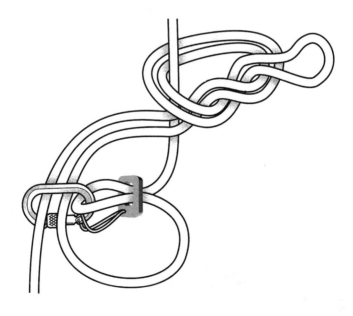

Introduction

A belay normally consists of a person who controls a rope which is secured to a climber and which can be locked off if the climber falls; when the rope is locked off, the fall is stopped. Components of a belay may include an anchor, the belayer, a belay plate or other device which locks off the rope which is secured to the climber, and the rope itself.

The simplest belay consists of a belayer holding a rope which is secured to the climber. The system works if the belayer is large, strong, is wearing gloves, if the climber is light and if the fall is short. Another term for belaying is lifelining.

On to the next system.

As climbers fell like flies, an improvement was made. The belayer led the rope around his body for more friction. To lock off after a fall, the belayer wrapped the rope around his leg on the brake-hand side (right side for right-handers). Same parameter requirements, fewer eulogies. Next system.

Hip Belays

Both the sitting hip belay and the standing hip belay (Figure 3–1) consist of a belayer who is secured to an anchor and a rope which is led behind the belayer's hips. For a right-hander, the right hand is the brake hand and is slid up and down the rope while gripping the rope at all times when on belay; the left hand is the guide hand.

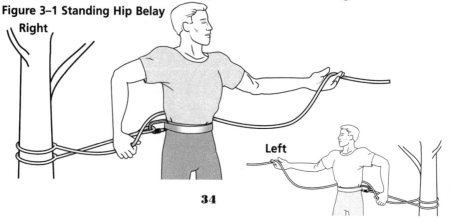

Figure 3–1 Standing Hip Belay

Right

Left

34

The anchor line is secured, adjusted and kept taut by the belayer. During a fall, the belayer grips both hands and moves his brake hand in front of his hip to increase friction and help stop the fall.

The anchor line is tied to the belayers swami belt or harness carabiner with a Bowline, Figure Eight Loop or the experienced climber's preference.

The Bowline (Figure 3–2) can be looped around a swami belt and doesn't require a carabiner.

Figure 3–2a Bowline
Right

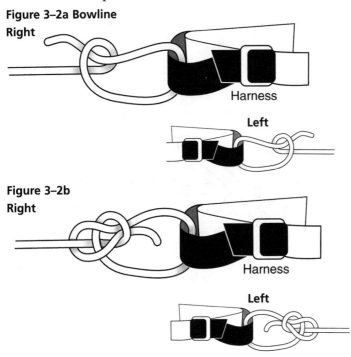

Harness

Left

Figure 3–2b
Right

Harness

Left

Using a harness carabiner, the Figure Eight Loop (Figure 3–3) can be tied in the bight and clipped to the 'biner. Without a carabiner, first tie a Figure Eight Knot in the standing part of the rope, then loop it around the belt and lead the free end back through the knot.

Figure 3–3a Figure Eight Loop
Right

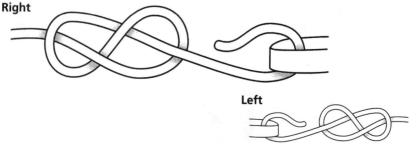

Left

Figure 3–3b
Right

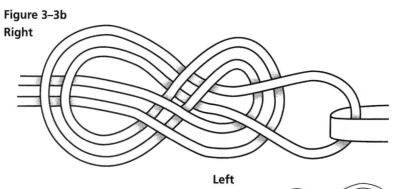

Left

The anchor line was illustrated as a single rope with loops tied to both the anchor and harness carabiner. The line could also be a doubled runner or a section of the climbing rope itself (Figure 3–4).

For an example of the latter, first tie a Bowline to the anchor, leaving enough free end to tie a second loop to the swami belt.

Figure 3–4 Interconnected Bowline

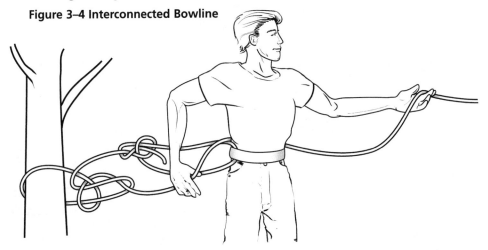

In addition to two interconnected Bowlines, the belayer may choose to interconnect two Figure Eight Loops, Mountaineering Bowlines, etc.

If there's a lot of slack in the climbing rope and the lead climber's anticipated pitch is short, another method used to

secure both the belayer and anchor with the climbing rope is to
first make a long bight in the rope. Then make a loop with a
Belayer's Hitch (Figure 3–5) in the end of the bight and clip in the
loop to a harness or swami belt carabiner; follow with a double-
line loop, also made using a Belayer's Hitch, and secure it to the
anchor.

**Figure 3–5a Belayer's Hitch
Right**

Left

**Figure 3–5b
Right**

Left

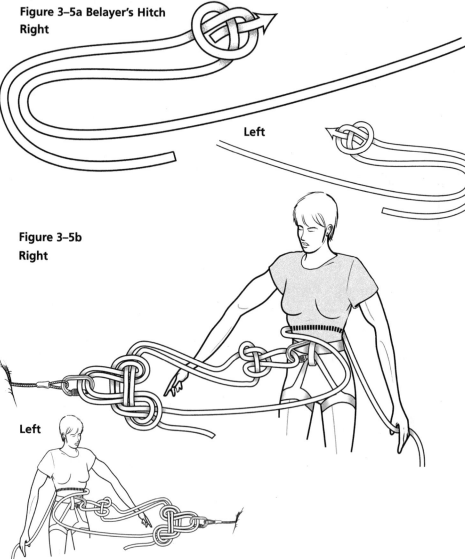

To save wear and tear (and burns) on clothing and on tissue,
several mechanical belay devices were designed.

The belay plate (Figure 3–6) is designed primarily for belaying the lead climber from below and secondarily for belaying the second climber from above. Some double-hole plates (i.e., those with 11mm holes) have also been used as rappel devices.

Make a bight in the climbing rope, insert the bight through the large hole in the plate and clip it off with a harness-carabiner (or two, with gates on opposite sides); plates come in different shapes (rectangular, circular, oval) and offer several hole combinations for belaying with a single rope, of the same or different diameters.

Figure 3–6 Belay Plate

Right

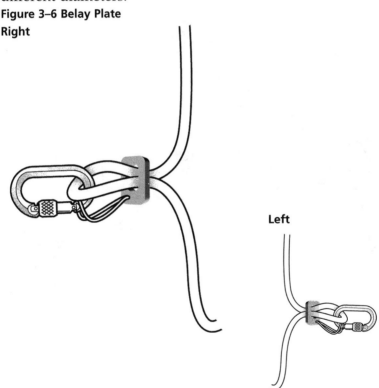

Left

The small line keeps the brake from sliding our of reach while paying out or taking in the rope. The brake hand (the right hand in the above illustration) should only be slid up and down the rope, never removed.

After a fall, the plate should be locked off as shown (Figure 3–7), leading a bight made in the lower, slack part of the rope (use the left hand to tie-off) through the carabiner and around the taut part of the rope and securing with an Overhand Knot (the keeper cord not shown, for clarity).

Figure 3–7 Locked-Off Belay Plate
Right

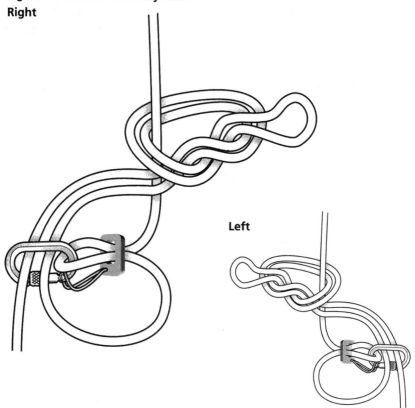

Left

The belayer can then transfer and secure the climbing rope to the anchor (using a French Prusik, Jumar, etc.) and escape the belay system to help the fallen climber.

Some belayer's lock off by simply tying an Overhand Loop in a bight of the slack part of the rope, butt against the plate.

After rigging the belay plate, some climbers also lead the brake rope (right-hand, slack part) around the waist for more friction in a modified hip belay.

Adjustable Anchor Tie-ins

There are occasions when an adjustable tie-in comes in handy. Two knots are widely used to accomplish such adjustability.

The first is the Clove Hitch (Figure 3–8), illustrated below.

Figure 3–8a Tie-in with Clove Hitch

Right

Left

Figure 3–8b

Right

Left

Clip the loops in a carabiner (Figure 3–8c).

Figure 3–8c

Right

Left

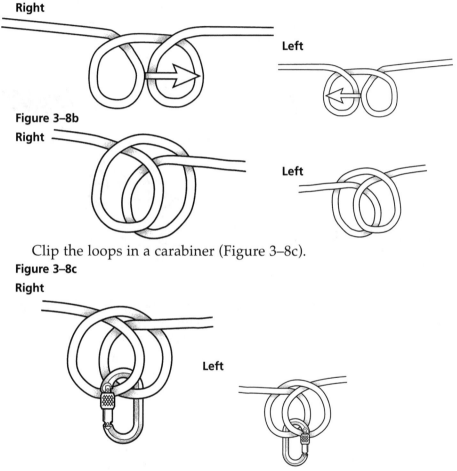

It is rigged as shown below.

Figure 3–9 Tie-in Rig

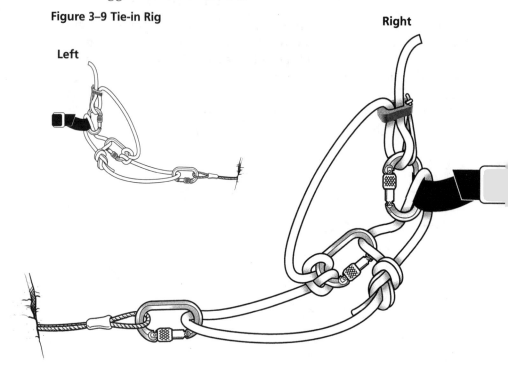

Adjust the Clove Hitch for a secure belay (correct anchor tension and direction in case of the climber's fall).

Instead of a Clove Hitch, a Belayer's Hitch (Figure 3–10) may be tied and the loop clipped in the anchorline carabiner (the same carabiner as was used with the Clove Hitch above).

Figure 3–10a Belayer's Hitch
Right

Figure 3–10b

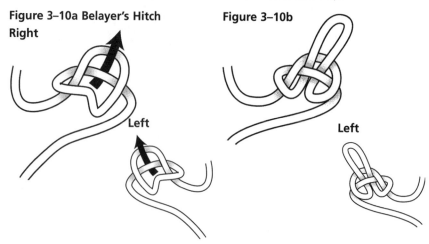

To tie-in an adjustable belay to a second anchor, simply throw a second Clove Hitch (or Belayer's Hitch) and clip it in the second anchor carabiner and adjust both hitches for correct belay tension and direction.

When a belay plate has been dropped or lost, an alternative is to use a carabiner rigged with a Munter Hitch (Figure 3–11). The hitch is a sliding friction knot which is used for both belaying (by both second climber and leader) and rappelling. The hitch is controversial, being hailed by some climbers and condemned by others.

It is two-directional and simple to make (a large pear-shaped carabiner helps to lessen rope twisting and knot jamming).

Figure 3–11 Munter Hitch

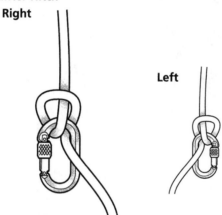

Again, the brake hand (right hand in the above illustration, gripping the lower, slack part of the rope) should only be slid up and down the rope, never removed.

Another alternative, one preferred by some climbers, is to use a Figure Eight Descender, normally used for rappelling (Figure 3–12). Use the small hole (often D-shaped, designed for belaying) for the main line and rig a keeper cord to keep the device from sliding out of reach while paying out or taking in the rope.

Figure 3–12 Figure Eight Descender

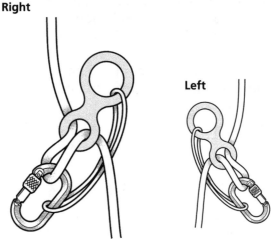

4

Mainline Knots

Introduction
Loops
    Overhand Loop
    Bowline
    Mountaineering Bowline
    FIGURE EIGHT LOOP (Figure Eight on a
      Bight, Guide Knot)
    Fisherman's Loop
    Bowline on a Bight
    THREE LOOP BOWLINE (Triple Bowline)
    Butterfly Knot
    LINEMAN'S LOOP (Butterfly Noose)
    Man-Harness Knot
    Rover Noose
Rope Wraps
    Bowline on a Coil
    Waist Loop
Bends
    OVERHAND BEND (Ring Bend, Tape Knot)
    FIGURE EIGHT BEND (Flemish Bend)
    FISHERMAN'S KNOT (Englishman's Knot)
    GRAPEVINE KNOT (Double Fisherman's Knot)
    BARREL KNOT (Triple Fisherman's Knot)
    Double Sheet Bend
    Carrick Bend
    HUNTER'S BEND (Rigger's Bend)

Introduction

Knots tied in the main climbing rope include knots used to secure the rope directly to the lead or second climber, loops used to secure the rope to an end climber's swami belt or harness, loops tied in the bight used to secure middle climbers, and bends used to join two ropes together (with the same or different diameters) to increase the length of the climbing rope.

Each knot should be dressed, set and tightened using bodyweight (and sometimes pliers). They should be tied and practiced at base camp, one-handed whenever possible. With eyes closed. While standing on one foot. In the rain. And wind. Amidst locusts.

Loops

The simplest loop, tied at the end of or in the middle of a rope, is the Overhand Loop (Figure 4–1).

Figure 4–1 Overhand Loop

Right

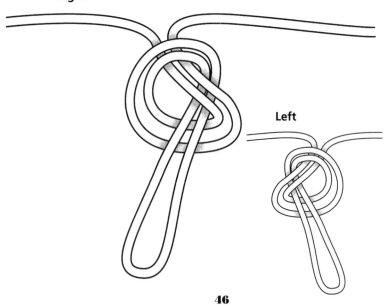

Left

The loop can also be used to bypass a section of line which is fraying and could possibly break. Simply tie it in the bight and include the bad section of line in the loop; under strain, the damaged section will be free of any pull.

The preferred knot for years was the Bowline (Figure 4–2), a non-slipping loop which could be fairly easily untied after loading. Set and tighten it by pulling on the standing part and both loop strands.

Figure 4–2a Bowline
Right

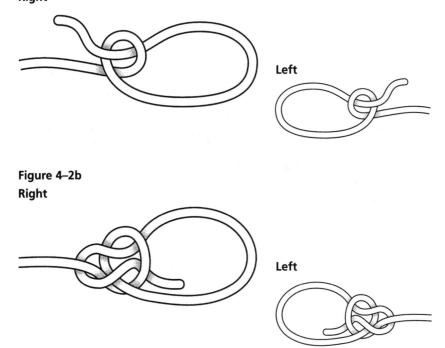

Left

Figure 4–2b
Right

Left

The Mountaineering Bowline (Figure 4–3) has an extra eye turn and is slightly stronger and more secure than the Bowline. It's also relatively easy to tie and untie, even after heavy and repeated strain and loading.

Figure 4–3a Mountaineering Bowline
Right

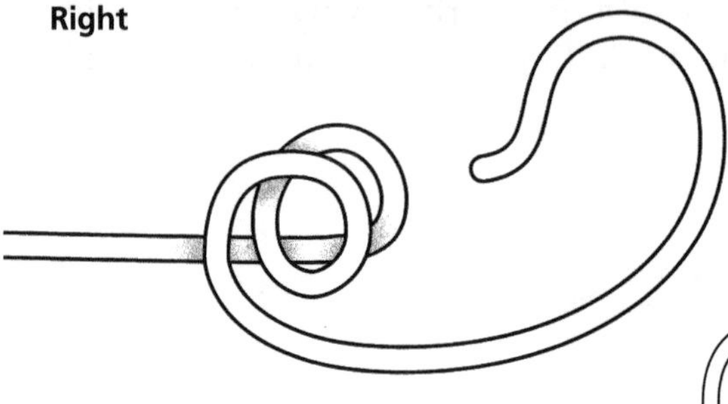

Left

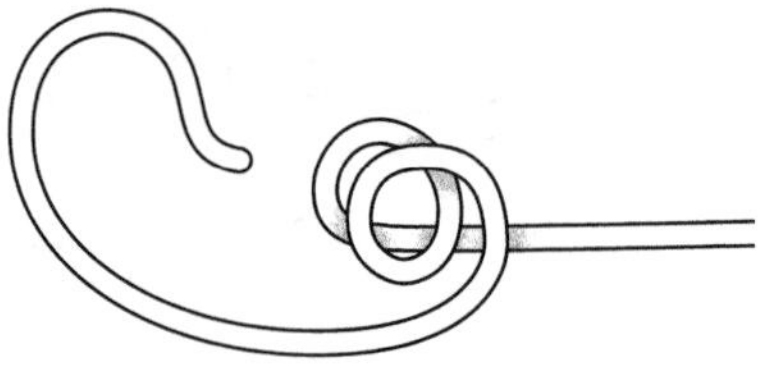

Figure 4–3b
Right

Left

Another preferred knot of many climbers is the Figure Eight Loop (Figure 4–4), also known as the Figure Eight on a Bight and as the Guide Knot. When securing to a swami belt or harness, tie a Figure Eight Knot in the standing part, then lead the free end around the belt and back through the knot.

Figure 4–4a Figure Eight Loop
Right

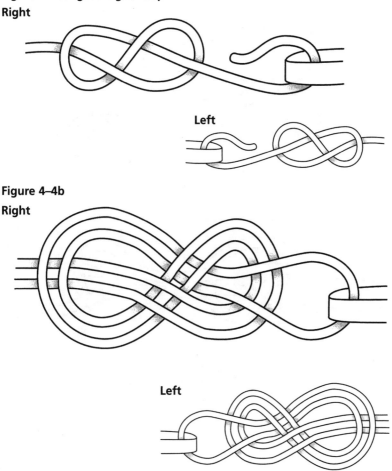

Left

Figure 4–4b
Right

Left

When tied in the bight, the loop can be used to secure a middle climber.

The Fisherman's Loop (Figure 4–5) has been used as an end climber's knot. It consists of a Fisherman's Knot with a loop. Tie it as shown, with the Overhand Knot in the standing part being tied first.

Figure 4–5a Fisherman's Loop
Right

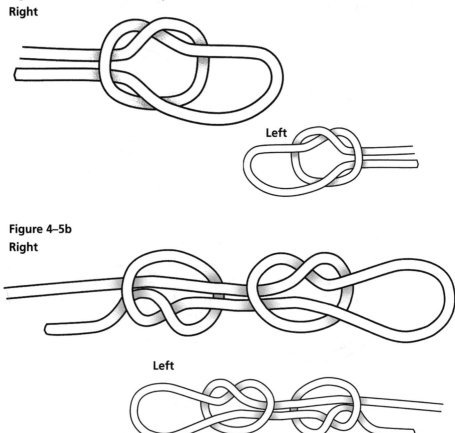

Left

Figure 4–5b
Right

Left

The Bowline on a Bight (figure 4–6) may be tied in the end of a rope or in the middle.

If used as a middle climber's knot, the double line can also be directly looped around the chest and is more comfortable than a single line loop.

Figure 4–6a Bowline on a Bight

Right

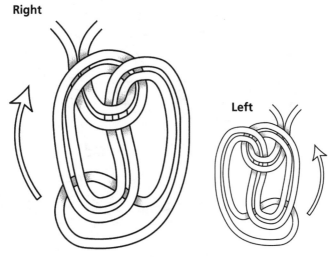

Left

Figure 4–6b

Right

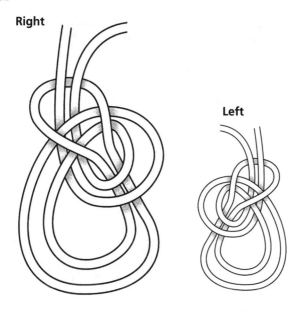

Left

Similarly, a Three Loop Bowline (Figure 4–7), also known as a Triple Bowline, results in a tripled line which may be looped over the head and around the chest. It may also be tied at the end of or in the middle of a rope.

Figure 4–7a Three Loop Bowline
Right

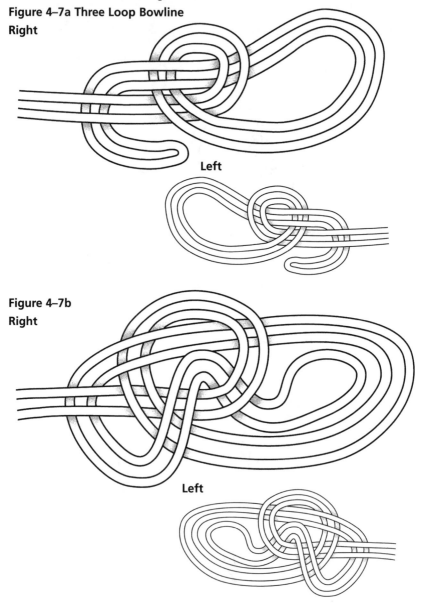

Left

Figure 4–7b
Right

Left

The Butterfly Knot (Figure 4–8), also known as an Alpine Butterfly, is used to secure a middle climber, mainly for traversing in terrain where the chance of a fall is remote.

It's also used to temporarily bypass a section of damaged rope (include it in the loop) and as a tie-in point.

Figure 4–8a Butterfly Knot

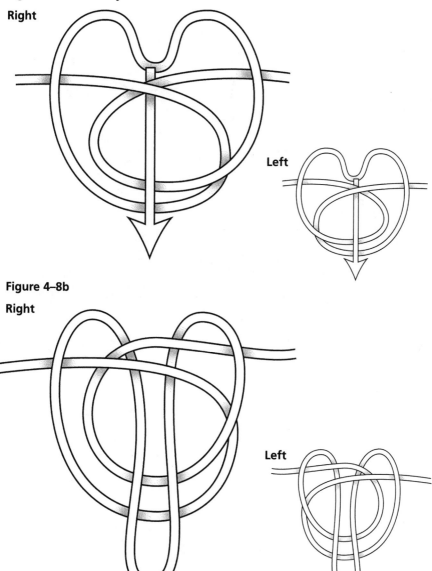

Right

Left

Figure 4–8b

Right

Left

The Lineman's Loop (Figure 4–9), also known as a Butterfly Noose or Lineman's Rider, is used as a middle climber's loop. It's compact, secure and is easy to tie and to loosen. When properly dressed, it doesn't jam easily and it holds equally well with a pull from either direction.

Figure 4–9a Lineman's Loop
Right

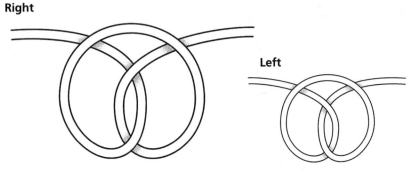

Left

Figure 4–9b
Right

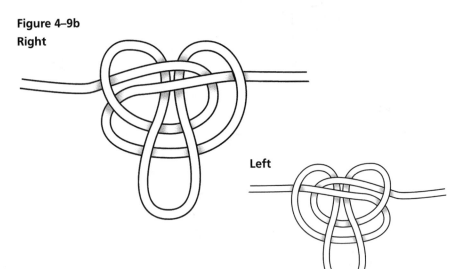

Left

Another middle climber's knot, the Man-Harness Knot (Figure 4–10), has already been introduced as the Belayer's Hitch. Dress and tighten it with bodyweight to prevent spilling.

Figure 4–10a Man-Harness Knot
Right

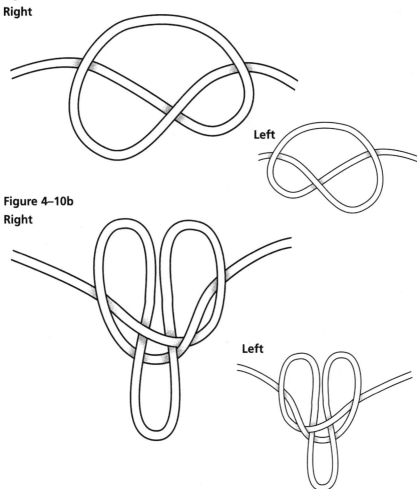

Left

Figure 4–10b
Right

Left

The Rover Noose (Figure 4–11) has been used as a middle climber's knot. It's tied in the bight and is another member of the figure eight family.

Figure 4–11a Rover Noose
Right

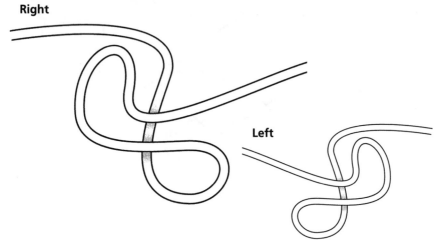

Left

Figure 4–11b
Right

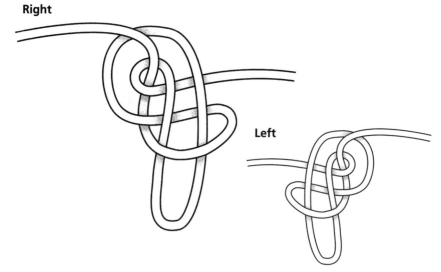

Left

Rope Wraps

The Bowline on a Coil (Figure 4–12) is used to secure a climber to a rope without a harness. Several turns of rope provide more comfort than a single, constricting turn.

However, a fall can cause pain and possibly severe internal organ and rib damage.

Figure 4–12a Bowline on a Coil

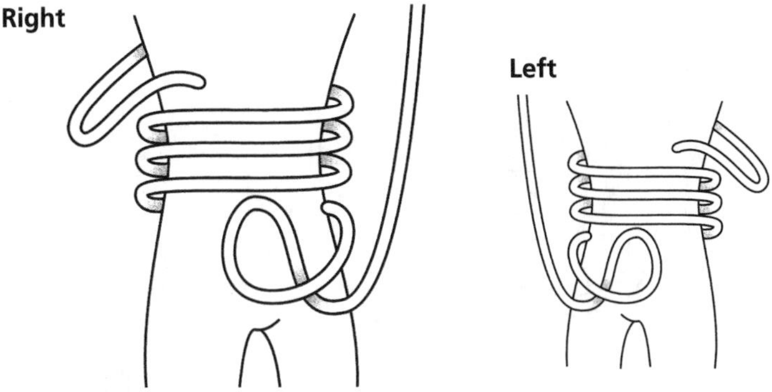

Right

Left

Figure 4–12b

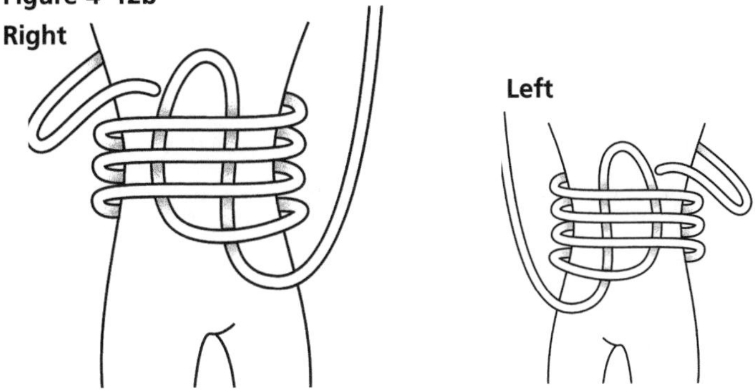

Right

Left

Figure 4–12c

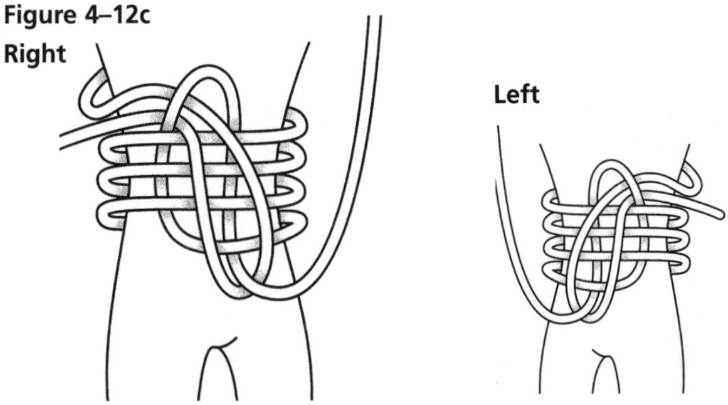

Right

Left

The Waist Loop (Figure 4–13) is used to secure a climber to a rope without a harness. Several turns of rope provide more comfort than a single, constricting one.

However, a fall can cause pain and possibly severe internal organ and rib damage.

Figure 4–13a Waist Loop
Right

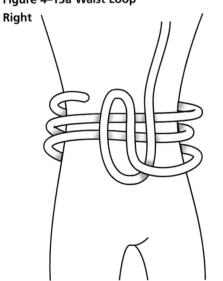

Left

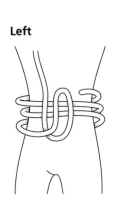

Figure 4–13b
Right

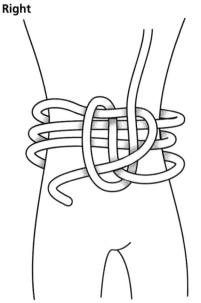

Left

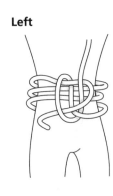

Bends

The Overhand Bend (Figure 4–14), also known as the Ring Bend, Tape Knot and by some as Water Knot, is used to join two ropes (of equal diameter) or webbings. It is used when the ropes are going to be subjected to an undue strain or an intermittent load; the strain is parallel to the two ropes and is more evenly distributed throughout the knot.

Tie an Overhand Knot in one of the ropes, then lead the end of the second rope back through the first knot.

Figure 4–14 Overhand Bend

Right

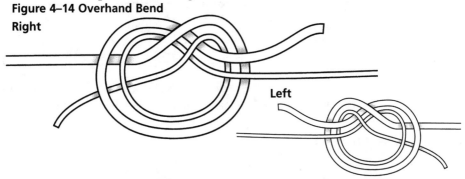

Left

The Figure Eight Bend (Figure 4–15), also called the Flemish Bend, is stronger and more secure than the Overhand Bend and is easier to untie after it has been under load.

Figure 4–15 Figure Eight Bend

Right

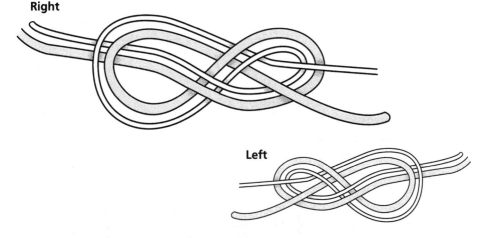

Left

The Fisherman's Knot (Figure 4–16), also known as the Englishman's Knot and by some as the Water Knot, has been used to tie two ropes of different materials together, such as a braided rope and a woven rope. However, it can work loose when tied with nylon ropes and must be secured.

Figure 4–16 Fisherman's Knot

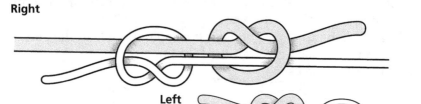

A better choice is the Grapevine Knot (Figure 4–17), also known as the Double Fisherman's Knot. Use bodyweight and pliers when setting and tightening the knot.

Figure 4–17 Grapevine Knot

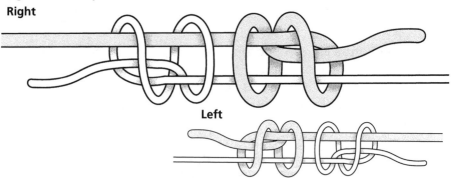

It's compact and is also used to form endless loops (slings) of rope; it's the preferred knot of many climbers when making prusik slings and when slinging a Jumar.

The Barrel Knot (Figure 4–18), also called the Triple Fisherman's Knot, is bulky but very strong.

Figure 4–18 Barrel Knot

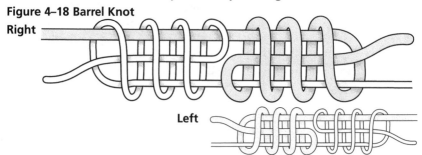

The Double Sheet Bend (Figure 4–19) is used to tie two ropes together which may vary considerably in diameter. It is also used when the ropes are wet or when using slick synthetic ropes.

Figure 4–19 Double Sheet Bend

Right

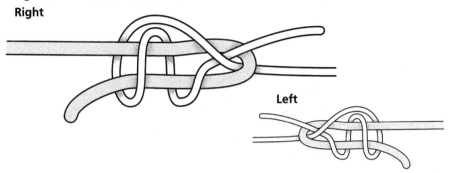

Left

The Sheet Bend (Figure 4–20) is shown below, for comparison. It's very versatile around the base camp but should not be used in a mainline.

Figure 4–20 Sheet Bend

Right

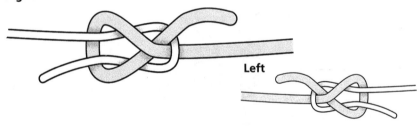

Left

The Carrick Bend (Figure 4-21) is used to join large, stiff ropes and can support very heavy loads. It doesn't jam and can be untied easily.

Figure 4–21 Carrick Bend

Right

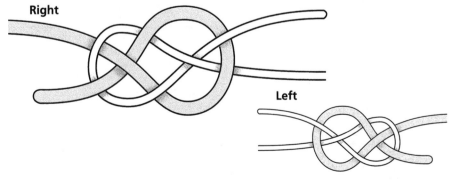

Left

The Hunter's Bend, or Rigger's Bend, is used to join lines of different diameters and different materials. It is effective when used with stiff or slippery synthetic ropes and is especially good with nylon ropes. Also, it doesn't distort and is easily untied.

Figure 4–22a Hunter's Bend
Right

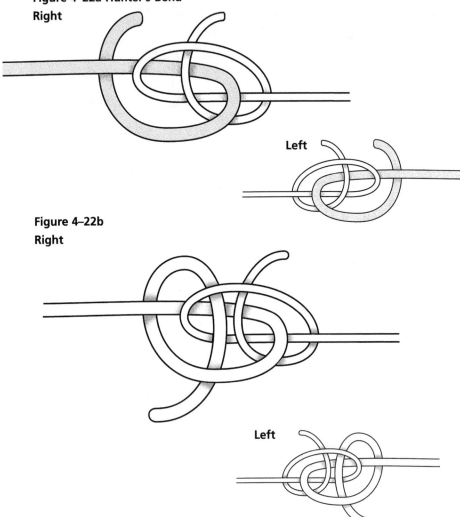

Left

Figure 4–22b
Right

Left

5

Harnesses and Slings

Introduction

Early climbers tied the climbing rope directly around their waist using a Figure Eight Loop, Bowline, etc. The single-turn loop was then replaced by multi-turn knots (e.g., Bowline on a Coil, Waist Loop) and multi-loop knots (e.g., Bowline on a Bight, French Bowline, etc.). Later came the swami belt, to be described shortly.

Harnesses were then developed, to improve safety and comfort, especially on long climbs.

Rope is still used but has been largely replaced by both flat and tubular webbing.

The basic sling is a simple length of rope or webbing, formed into an endless loop with the ends secured by an Overhand Bend (Ring Bend, Tape Knot, Water Knot) or a Grapevine Knot (Double Fisherman's Knot). Many commercially available slings have the ends sewn together.

The chapter presents knots and rigging used to make harnesses and auxiliary climbing devices. It concludes with several knots used in emergency and rescue work.

The swami belt (Figure 5–1) is used in belay systems, prusiking and rappelling and consists of a single length of one or

Figure 5–1a Swami Belt with Overhand Bend

Right

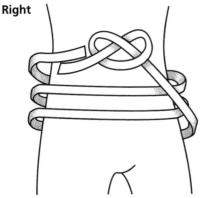

Left

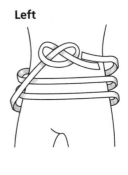

two inch webbing wrapped around the waist five or six times (only three shown, for clarity); the ends are secured by an Overhand Bend.

Figure 5–1b

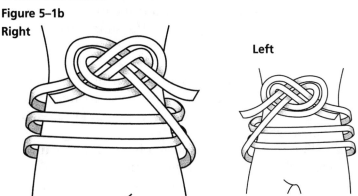

The climbing rope is either tied directly to the belt (e.g., Figure Eight Loop, Bowline, etc.) or is tied to a locking carabiner which is secured around the belt.

Several turns of webbing provide more comfort than a single, constricting rope around the waist while climbing.

However, a fall can cause pain and possibly severe internal organ and rib damage.

The belt can be combined with a sling to add supporting leg loops.

Seat Slings

The Seat Sling(Figure 5–2) is normally used in conjunction with a modified body rappel (Seat Sling Dulfer) or with a rappel device

Figure 5–2 Seat Sling

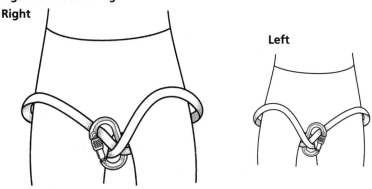

(e.g., Figure Eight Descender), although there are other applications when it is combined with and connected to a chest harness or swami belt, e.g., prusiking or belaying.

The sling consists of a single length of rope or webbing with the ends secured by an Overhand Bend (a sling fitted with a buckle is easier to adjust). Loop the sling as shown and clip a carabiner to the cross in the figure eight.

To lessen heat from climbing rope friction and to improve security, use two 'biners with gates set in opposite directions.

As the sling is constructed of but a single loop, failure at any point could be catastrophic.

The Diaper Sling (Figure 5–3) is normally used in conjunction with a modified body rappel (Seat Sling Dulfer) or with a rappel device (e.g., Figure Eight Descender), although there are other applications when it is combined with and connected to a chest harness or swami belt, e.g., prusiking or belaying.

The sling consists of a single length of rope or webbing with the ends secured by an Overhand Bend (a sling fitted with a buckle is easier to adjust). Loop the sling as shown, with the knot behind and in the small of the back.

Figure 5–3 Diaper Sling
Right

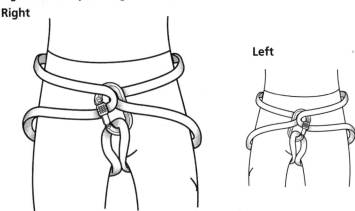

Left

The three bights are clipped in a locking carabiner (when used in a modified body rappel, two 'biners are better, to dissipate more heat from the rope friction).

As the sling is constructed of but a single loop, failure at any point could be catastrophic.

The Oversized Diaper Sling (Figure 5–4) is normally used in conjunction with a modified body rappel (Seat Sling Dulfer) or with a rappel device (e.g., Figure Eight Descender), although there are other applications when it is combined with and connected to a chest harness or swami belt, e.g., prusiking or belaying.

The sling consists of a single length of rope or webbing with the ends secured by an Overhand Bend (a sling fitted with a buckle is easier to adjust). Loop the sling, with the knot behind and in the small of the back.

The sling is similar and superior to the Diaper Sling. It is easier to rig, is more comfortable and causes less stress to the carabiner which is clipped to the two bights as shown.

Figure 5–4 Oversized Diaper Sling

Right

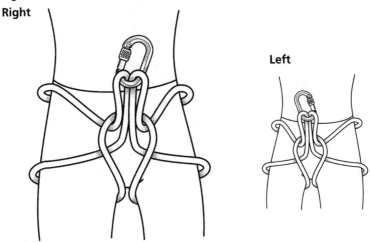

Left

However, it is still a single loop and failure at any point could be catastrophic.

The Diaper Seat Sling (Figure 5–5) is normally used in conjunction with a modified body rappel (Seat Sling Dulfer) or with a rappel device (e.g., Figure Eight Descender), although there are other applications when it is combined with and connected to a chest harness or swami belt, e.g., prusiking or belaying.

The sling consists of a single length of rope or webbing with the ends secured by an Overhand Bend (a sling fitted with a buckle is easier to adjust).

Figure 5–5 Diaper Seat Sling

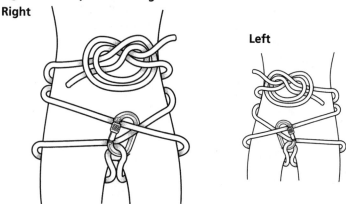

One can use two carabiners to dissipate more heat.

The sling is constructed of a single loop and failure at any point could be catastrophic.

The G.I. Rig (Figure 5–6) is normally used in conjunction with a modified body rappel (Seat Sling Dulfer) or with a rappel device (e.g., Figure Eight Descender), although there are other applications when it is combined with and connected to a chest harness or swami belt, e.g., prusiking or belaying.

The sling consists of a single length of rope or webbing with the ends secured by an Overhand Bend (a sling fitted with a buckle is easier to adjust).

Loop the sling as shown; for a right-handed climber, the midpoint of the rope or webbing should be on the left side (control hand) and the securing Overhand Bend on the right side (brake hand).

Figure 5–6a G.I. Rig
Right

Left

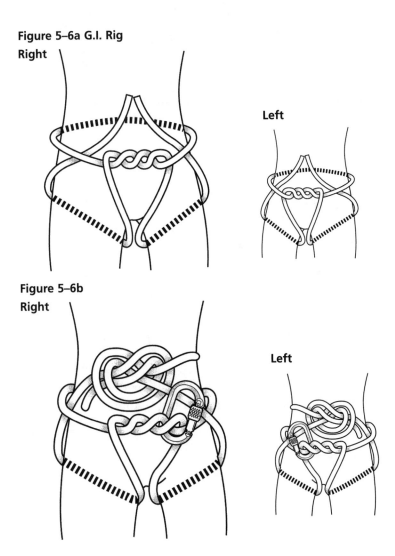

Figure 5–6b
Right

Left

Clip both waist rope loops in a locking carabiner (when used in a modified body rappel, two 'biners are better, to dissipate more heat from the climbing rope friction).

As the sling is constructed of but a single loop, failure at any point could be catastrophic.

Chest Harnesses

The One-Line Chest Harness (Figure 5–7) is made with a single length of rope or webbing. Tie a Bowline in one end of the line, leaving a foot or two of the free end. Lead the wrapping end of the line around the center of the chest from one to several times, leaving about a four foot end.

Figure 5–7a One-Line Chest Harness

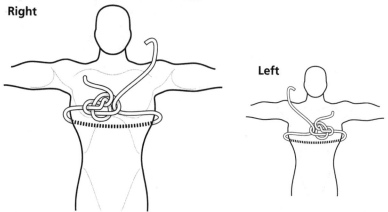

Lead the end through the central loop, over the left shoulder and down under the back of the chest loop(s), then back over the right shoulder. Tie the two ends with an Overhand Bend. Then clip the front chest loops with a carabiner.

Figure 5–7b

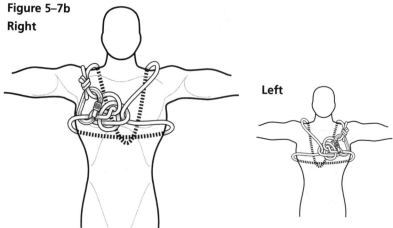

The harness consists of but a single line and failure at any point could be catastrophic.

The Two-Line Chest Harness (Figure 5–8) is begun by tying a Bowline in the climbing rope at the center of and around the chest.

Figure 5–8 Two-Line Chest Harness

Right

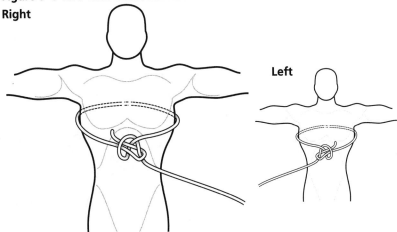

Left

The second, lighter rope or webbing is used (Figure 5–8b) mainly to keep the central loop from slipping down the chest. Secure it with Two Half Hitches in the front, a Girth Hitch in the back and Two Half Hitches in the front, as shown.

Figure 5–8b

Right

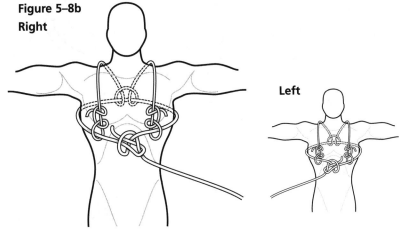

Left

The Safety Harness (Figure 5–9) is made in the end of a climbing rope or safety line. Arrange the rope as shown below. The rope in the bight from a to b should be long enough to go from the right hip, over the left shoulder and down to the left hip.

Figure 5–9a Saftey Harness

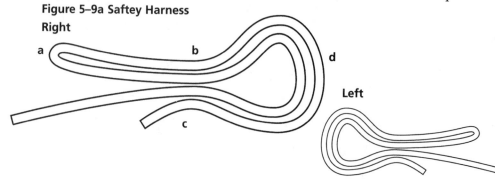

Take all four strands between b and c in one hand and tie an Overhand Loop Knot (Figure 5–9b).

Figure 5–9b

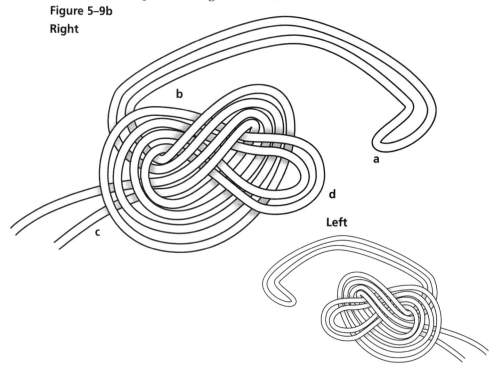

Wrap the harness over the left shoulder and around the back as shown, holding the double strand loop in the right hand and the single strand loop in the left hand.

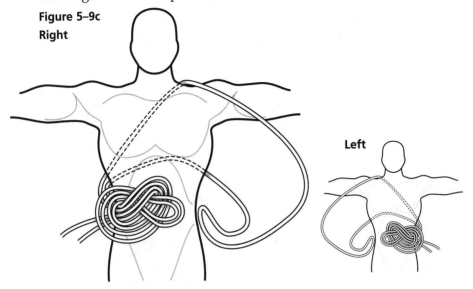

Figure 5–9c
Right

Left

Lead the single loop through the double loop (Figure 5–9d), insert the left hand through the single loop, then pull it with the right hand up over the left arm, the left shoulder and over the head to the right shoulder.

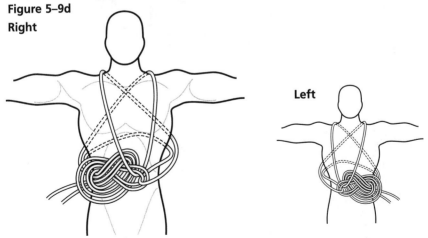

Figure 5–9d
Right

Left

Adjust the harness.

**Figure 5–10
Etrier**

Auxiliary Slings

**Figure 5–10
Etrier**

An Etrier (Figure 5–10) is a step ladder normally constructed of one-inch, flat webbing. Formerly made of rope, it may have from two to five one-foot steps (a four-step etrier is illustrated requiring fifteen feet of webbing).

The small loop, or eye, at the top is made by tying a Frost Knot (Figure 5–11), an Overhand Knot tied with three strands of webbing (the triple overlapped section is about ten inches long):

Figure 5–11a Frost Knot

Right

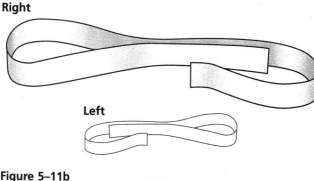

Left

Figure 5–11b

Right

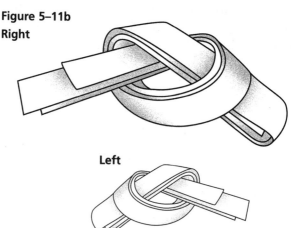

Left

Then tie three Overhand Knots to construct the four steps; leave enough webbing before dressing and setting each knot so that the top three stirrups are somewhat horizontal and wide enough for the shoe or boot.

Figure 5–12 Aider

Etriers are normally used in pairs, e.g., when a lead climber is placing protection; after placing an anchor, the leader attaches the etriers to the anchor with carabiners, climbs the steps and places the next protection.

A pair of etriers may be used instead of foot loops to prusik; don't forget to chicken loop each ankle.

A single etrier and Jumar, Prusik Knot, etc., may be hooked to the climbing rope above a lip edge which is difficult to negotiate. It may also be used in a haul system; leg muscles pushing down are stronger and more enduring than arm and shoulder muscles pulling up.

A Subaider, or a subsidiary etrier, is a one-half inch, two step sling which is tied in the eye of an etrier (lead the webbing through the eye and tie the ends with an Overhand Bend; then tie an Overhand Knot in the middle of the sling, forming two loops); the combination of an etrier and a subaider is called an Aider (Figure 5–12):

The subaider portion is used as a tether (eliminating the need for a Daisy Chain) to a swami belt or seat harness while placing protection or as a back-up safety line when prusiking with aiders. The two loops may also be used as the top two steps of a ladder when using a single aider to place protection, a deviation, etc.

The Foot Loop (Figure 5–13) assembly consists of a stirrup, in which to put a foot, and a connecting line (rope or webbing) whose end is connected to either a prusik device (e.g., Jumar) or to the climbing rope (by means of a Prusik Knot, Ascender Knot, etc.).

Figure 5–13 Foot Loop

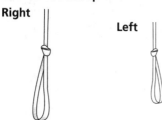

When prusiking or downclimbing, a chicken loop should be used with each foot loop, both to keep the foot in the stirrup and to support the climber by the ankle in the event of an upper attachment failure.

Chicken Loops

A chicken loop should serve two purposes. First, it should help hold the foot in the stirrup of a foot loop while prusiking or downclimbing (or in the step of an etrier or aider which is being used to ascend or descend with friction knots or devices). Second, it should be able to hold the climber by the ankle in the event of an upper attachment failure and a resulting fall or inversion.

The simplest is the Sewn Chicken Loop (Figure 5–14), or Endless Chicken Loop, which is a simple sling. Put it on before slipping into a boot; it should slip over the foot and sock but not over a boot or shoe.

Figure 5–14 Sewn Chicken Loop

A similar chicken loop is the Ganter Chicken Loop (Figure 5–15), a short length of webbing or rope with a loop at each end; the ends are secured by a carabiner (the chicken loop need not be rigged before putting on a shoe or boot).

Figure 5–15 Ganter Chicken Loop

Right  Left

Another similar loop is the Buckled Chicken Loop, a short sling which is closed with a buckle. Some foot loops already have a chicken loop sewn in the assembly.

A Smart Chicken Loop (Figure 5–16) assembly consists of an interconnecting foot loop, stirrup and chicken loop.

Figure 5–16 Smart Chicken Loop

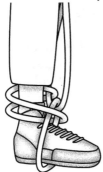

A Cinch Knot Chicken Loop (Figure 5–17) assembly consists of a foot loop and a chicken loop but may not hold a climber is he becomes inverted:

Figure 5–17 Cinch Knot Chicken Loop

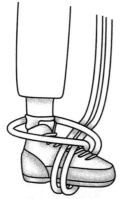

Relief Straps (Figure 5–18) consist of two foot stirrups (one can suffice) which are attached to a seat harness. They are used when one may have to spend a lot of time in the harness, e.g., on long traverses or rappels or while working in midair. Standing in them helps to restore blood circulation in the legs and takes pressure off constricting harnesses.

Figure 5–18 Relief Straps

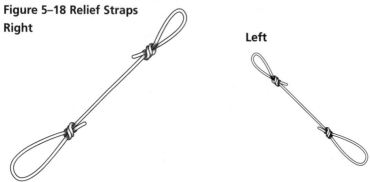

Right

Left

A Daisy Chain (Figure 5–19) consists of several carabiners which are linked together (the end link preferred by some climbers is a Fifi Hook). It is used as a tether in aid climbing and facilitates the placements of pieces of protection, especially on near-vertical walls and overhangs. The Fifi Hook (or a carabiner) is hooked around the anchor and the other end of the chain is secured to a seat harness.

Figure 5–19 Daisy Chain with Fifi Hook

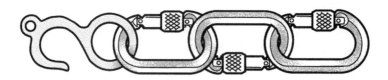

Safety Slings

The French Bowline (Figure 5–20) is used in emergency rescue work and when lowering a person to perform a hazardous but necessary task.

The knot is similar to the Bowline, the difference being that the free end is led through the beginning eye twice, instead of once, before passing around the standing part and back down through the eye to finish the knot.

Two loops are thus formed, loosely connected through the eye: a seat sling and an arm pit loop. The weight of a person sitting in the sling hauls the loop taut, keeping the person relatively safe against falling out, and held fast if unconscious.

Extreme caution is necessary and advised when using this knot; check and recheck it before using.

Figure 5–20 French Bowline

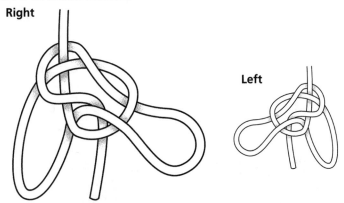

Right

Left

The Portuguese Bowline (Figure 5–21) has also been used to support a person being raised or lowered to safety, but the French Bowline is preferred. Both loops are adjustable in size.

Figure 5–21a Portuguese Bowline

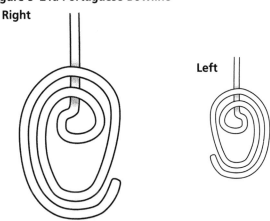

Right

Left

Figure 5–21b
Right

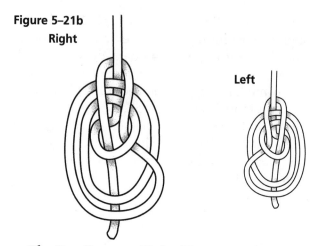

Left

The Bowline on a Bight (Figure 5–22) is also used in emergency rescue work. It's more difficult to adjust the two loops than with the French or Portuguese Bowlines.

Figure 5–22a Bowline on a Bight
Right

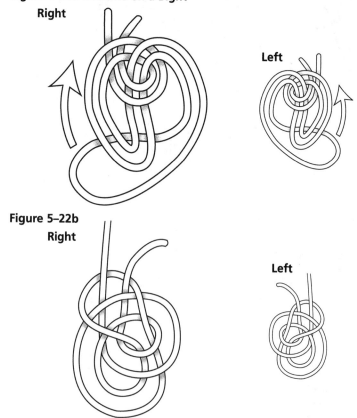

Left

Figure 5–22b
Right

Left

The Spanish Bowline (Figure 5–23) is used when an improvised seat sling and arm pit loop are needed. It is begun by forming a Slip Knot; after a little rope origami, the variable sized loops are finished.

Figure 5–23a Spanish Bowline

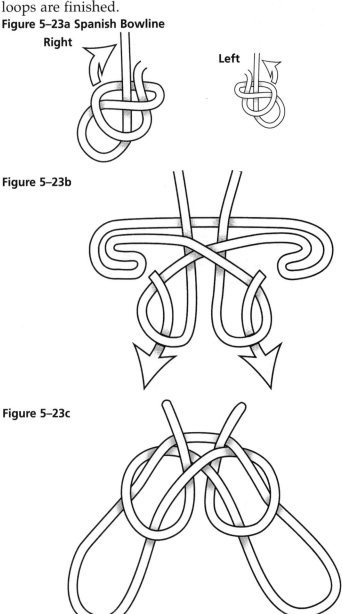

Right

Left

Figure 5–23b

Figure 5–23c

The Three Loop Bowline (Figure 5–24), also known as the Triple Bowline, consists of three loops, two of which can be adjusted against each other.

If points A and B are joined (stage two of the illustration), and a hook, carabiner or another rope is looped through point X, the knots junction can be used to provide four lifting loops for attaching an emergency rescue litter. Extreme caution is necessary and recommended. The various loops, and the victim, must be secured.

Figure 5–24a Three Loop Bowline
Right

Left

Figure 5–24b
Right

a
b

x

Left

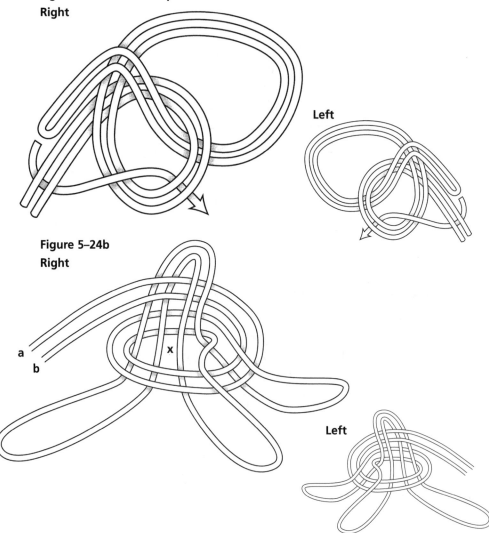

Prusik and Rappel Knots

Introduction

To prusik is to climb a rope using friction knots which grip the rope or using one-way mechanical camming devices (e.g., Jumars) which clamp the rope. The knots and devices are connected to foot stirrups by slings and carabiners. In a simple two-foot system, all of one's weight is put on one foot while standing in one of the foot stirrups; then the knot or device connected to the second foot stirrup is slid up the rope and the climber shifts all his weight onto the second foot stirrup, removing his weight from the first. He then slides the first knot up the rope. And so on. The climber alternately shifts his weight from one stirrup to the other and then slides the opposite friction knot or mechanical device up the rope.

Downclimbing is the reverse of prusiking. Alternately shift weight from one foot to the other and slide the opposite knot or device down the rope.

To rappel is to slide down in a controlled manner. Control is maintained by using friction, generated either by contact between the rope and the climber's body or between the rope and a mechanical descending device, or both.

There are occasions when a climber needs to change from a rappel to a prusik, or vice versa, e.g., rappelling down a rope to a point where the climber stops (i.e., locks off) and photographs some feature of a crag, eagles nest, etc., sometimes from an otherwise inaccessible vantage point. After finishing the project, the climber changes over to a prusik, unlocks the rappel and prusiks back up the rope. The general name for the various techniques is changeover.

If the climbing rope consists of two or more ropes joined by knots, the climber will have to crossover each knot while descending, which involves changing over from rappel to prusik (or downclimb) and then back to rappel.

Changeovers and crossovers are needed to get past knots, anchors, deviations, obstacles and when changing from one rope to another.

84

The chapter presents prusik and rappel knots and rigging. It concludes with a section on pull-downs, i.e., various methods for retrieving the climbing rope from an anchor after a rappel.

Prusik Knots

The Prusik Knot (Figure 6–1), also known as a Vertical Stop Hitch, is used when climbing a vertical rope or near-vertical traverse. It provides a camming, ratchet or clamping action when under weight but slides along the rope easily and smoothly when not weighted. Other applications include the knot being used as a self-belay while rappelling, escaping a belay system in order to help after a leader has fallen, holding a safety sling while crossing a knot (or deviation) in a long drop, securing a climber when changing over from rappelling to prusiking or from prusiking to rappelling, etc.

When climbing a kernmantle rope (or a right-laid stranded rope), the right-handed version of the knot is tied as shown:

Figure 6–1a Prusik Knot

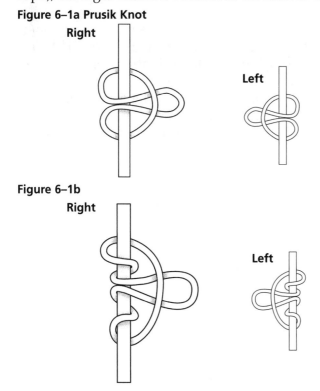

Right

Left

Figure 6–1b

Right

Left

For increased friction, the prusik cord should be of smaller diameter than that of the climbing rope; it should also be supple and non-stretch.

For heavier climbers or when the climbing rope may get wet (e.g., near a waterfall), make three or more wraps instead of two.

For left-laid rope, the knot should be tied as shown (Figure 6–2):

Figure 6–2 Left-Handed Prusik Knot

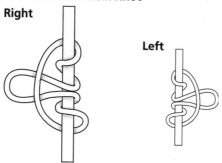

Right

Left

Once tied and set, the foot loop slings (or etriers), safety lines, etc., are secured to the prusik loops with Girth Hitches, carabiners, etc. When prusiking or downclimbing, use a chicken loop around each ankle to keep feet secured in the stirrups.

Webbing can and has been used to make Prusik Knots; it normally takes an extra wrap or two to provide enough friction for a tight grip and the knot is more difficult to break and to loosen.

The Three Coil Prusik Knot (Figure 6–3) slides upward more easily than a standard Prusik Knot, an advantage on a long prusik climb. The top part of the knot provides more friction and grip than the bottom coil of the knot.

The knot is shown below; the free ends should be secured by an Overhand Bend.

Figure 6–3 Three Coil Prusik Knot

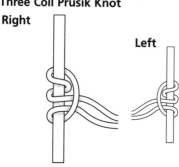

Right

Left

A four (or more) coil knot (Figure 6–4) provides even more friction:

Figure 6–4 Four Coil Prusik Knot

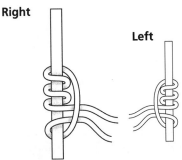

When a climber's hands are cold and wet, the Prusik Knot can be difficult to grip, break or loosen. Adding a carabiner (rectangular shape the best) to a friction wrap has been successful in streamlining the upward movement of the knot. The assembly is called a Bachman Knot (Figure 6–5).

Figure 6–5 Bachmann Knot

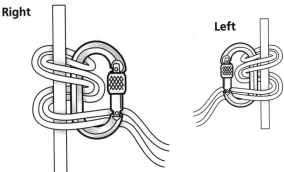

The assembly has largely been replaced by a Jumar (which itself has not been dropped or lost and needs a temporary replacement).

The Ascender Knot (Figure 6–6), a helical knot closely related to the French Prusik, has the same applications as a Prusik Knot but also has some advantages over the Prusik; it slides more easily while not loaded, wraps can be added or subtracted without having to remove a harness, foot loop or anchor sling, and the knot can be released under load. A disadvantage is that downward pressure on the top coil of the knot can break it, even if it is under load; if a top ascender slides down and contacts a lower ascender, one may end up descending instead of ascending, rapidly.

The knot is shown, tied off with a Bowline; five to ten wraps are normally made, depending on the weight of the climber, whether the rope is wet or muddy, etc. To test the knot, hold the bottom of the knot and pull upward on the climbing rope; it had better hold, or more wraps must be added.

Figure 6–6 Ascender Knot

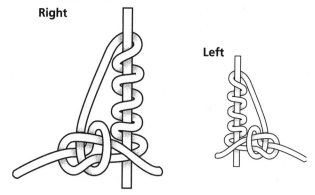

The French Prusik (Figure 6–7), a helical knot closely related to the Ascender Knot, has the same applications as a Prusik Knot but also has some advantages over the Prusik; it slides more easily while not loaded and can be released under load. A disadvantage is that downward pressure on the top coil of the knot can break it, even if it is under load; if a top ascender slides down and contacts a lower ascender, one may end up descending instead of ascending, rapidly.

Two applications are common, one around a carabiner and another around a Swami Belt; five to ten wraps are normally made, depending on the weight of the climber, whether the rope is wet or muddy, etc. To test the knot, hold the bottom of the knot and pull upward on the climbing rope; it had better hold, or more wraps must be added.

Figure 6–7 French Prusik

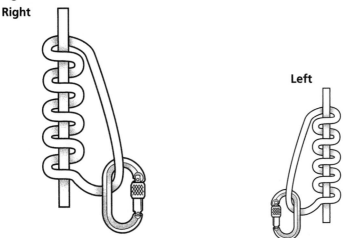

The Klemheist Knot (Figure 6–8), also known as a Headon Knot, is a variation of the Prusik Knot; it is easier to tie, even one-handed, and works with both rope and webbing.

Figure 6–8 Klemheist Knot

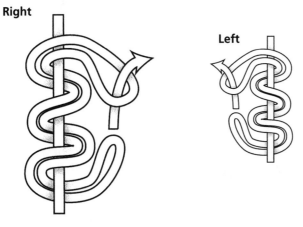

The Hedden Knot (Figure 6–9), also known as a Kreuzklem Knot, is a variation of the Figure Eight, Ascender and Prusik Knots. It works best with webbing slings.

Figure 6–9a Hedden Knot
Right

Left

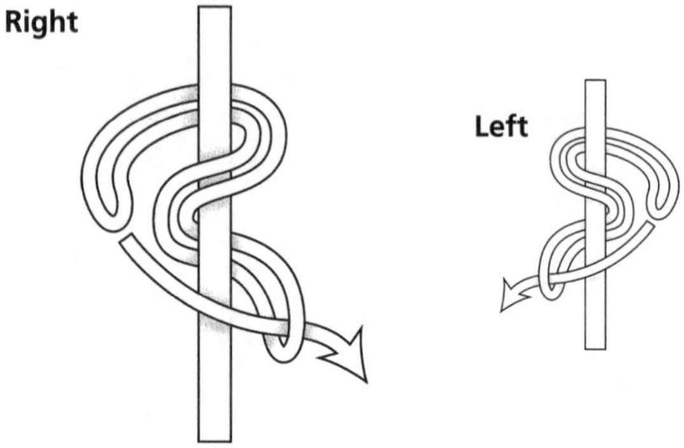

Figure 6–9b
Right

Left

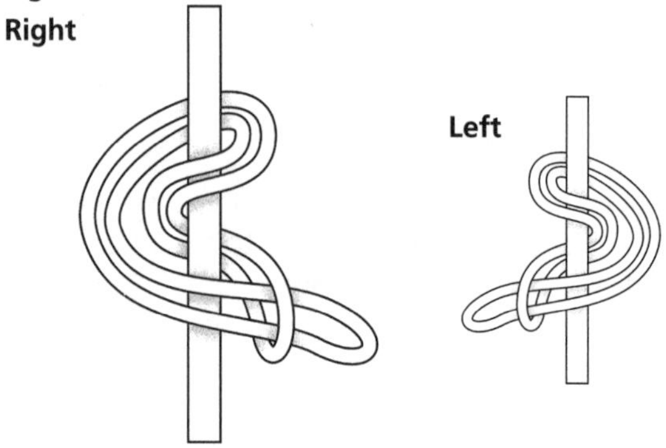

Rappels

The rigging for a Body Rappel (Figure 6–10), also known as a Dulfer Rappel, is shown for a right-handed rappeller (the right hand is for braking, the left hand for balance):

Keep the right leg slightly behind the left leg to help prevent the rope from creeping down the leg, unwrapping and upsetting the rappeller.

Padding for the leg and shoulder and gloves for the hands lessen abrasions and rope burns; the rappel is also called the Hot Seat Rappel.

Figure 6–10 Body Rappel
Right

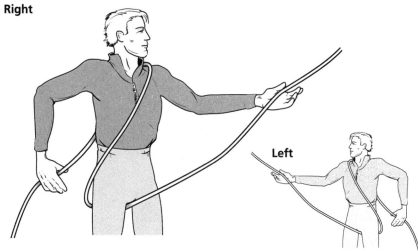

Left

To lessen seat discomfort and eliminate leg burns, add a seat sling to the rigging; the modified rappel is then known as a Seat Sling Dulfer (Figure 6–11) and the simplest example is shown (some climbers used two carabiners with gates set in opposite directions):

Figure 6–11 Seat Sling Dulfer
Right

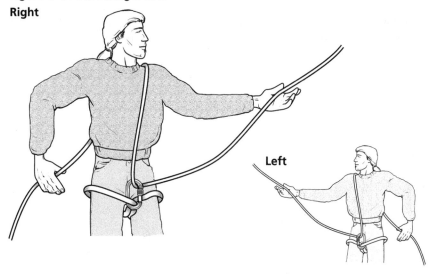

Left

On a short, moderately steep slope where a handline can be rigged, it is more efficient to use the Hasty Rappel (Figure 6–12) or Double Arm Rappel, shown below (protective clothing and gloves helpful):

Figure 6–12 Hasty Rappel

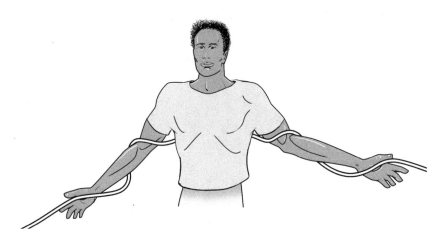

The Figure 8 Descender (Figure 6–13a) is a fixed friction rappel device, although it is also used and preferred by some as a belay device.

Lead a bight of the climbing rope through the large hole and around and under the back of the descender. Then clip in a locking carabiner in the smaller hole (some climbers prefer two carabiners with the gates opposite each other); the small hole is often D-shaped and is used when the device is rigged for belaying. The carabiner(s) is clipped to a swami belt, seat harness, etc.

Figure 6–13a Figure 8 Descender

Right

Left

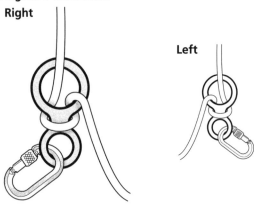

To lock off the device and stop the rappel (Figure 6–13b), jam the brake hand rope under the control hand rope against the descender.

Figure 6–13b Figure 8 Descender-Locked Off

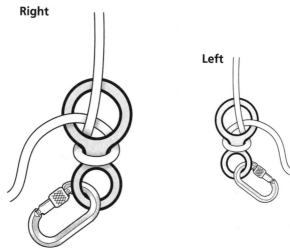

To completely lock off the device (e.g., during a changeover or crossover to a prusik or downclimb), lead a bight of the slack brake rope (with the left hand) through the large hole in the descender and tie it off around the top, taut portion of the rope with an Overhand Knot.

The Straight 8 Descender (Figure 6–14) has a squared-off shape and provides added friction; it is a little more difficult to lock off than the Figure 8 Descender.

Figure 6–14 Straight 8 Descender

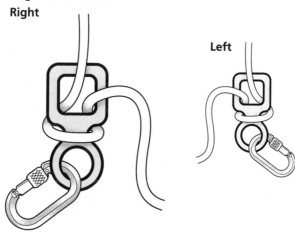

A disadvantage (Figure 6–15) with both devices is that they must be removed from the harness in order to rig them. Another drawback is that in some circumstances the rope can become girth hitched around the device and locked in place, necessitating a prusik to break the hitch.

Figure 6-15 Jammed Figure 8 Descender

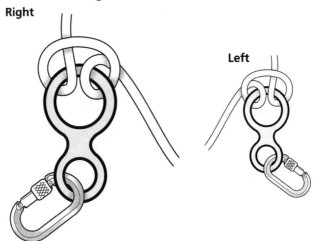

The Rescue 8 Descender (Figure 6–16) was designed to eliminate the problem. It can be rigged as above for normal use or as below when extra friction is needed.

Figure 6–16 Rescue 8 Descender

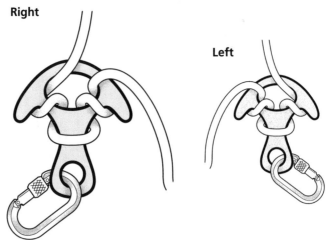

Carabiner brakes have been and continue to be used for rappelling and belaying. They are rough on the rope, the carabiners and on a spinning rappeller. In addition, they require more hardware than may be convenient to carry and are difficult to rig when fatigued, cold or in darkness. Also, since carabiners are designed to load on their long axis and since the gates are side-loaded in a rappel or belay, the gates will eventually cease to open and close smoothly, it at all.

A Carabine Wrap (Figure 6–17) consists of several wraps of the climbing rope around and through a carabiner, as shown (harness carabiner(s) not shown):

Figure 6–17 Carabiner Wrap

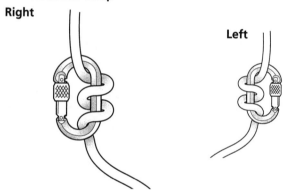

Right

Left

The wrap will wear out carabiners, kink ropes and spin rappellers.

To lessen spin, a simple one-bar brake (Figure 6–18) can be used (not shown is the carabiner(s) which clips the brake to a swami belt, seat harness, etc.):

Figure 6–18 Carabiner Brake

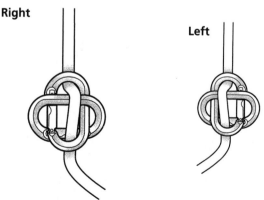

Right

Left

It consist of two carabiners, one of them placed around the other to serve as a cross-bar (some climbers prefer to use four 'biners, two cross-bars around the second pair).

All carabiner gates should be oriented so that the rope cannot open them.

An additional carabiner can provide more friction (Figure 6–19):

Figure 6–19 Carabiner Brake with Three 'Biners

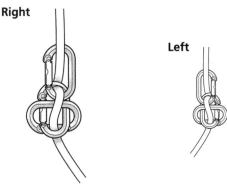

In the single Carabiner Brake, with four carabiners, a third cross-carabiner could be added for more friction, but most often used is the Double Carabiner Brake (Figure 6–20) (harness carabiner(s) not shown):

Figure 6–20 Double Carabiner Brake

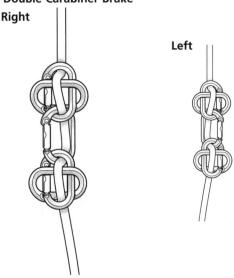

If a second connecting-link carabiner is added, it's called a Six Carabiner Brake by mountaineers.

Some climbers rig additional cross-bar 'biners in the brake, others add more longitudinal ones, etc.

The Munter Hitch (Figure 6–21), also known as an Italian Hitch, is a sliding friction knot which has been used for both belaying (by both second climber and leader) and rappelling; it is controversial, being used with confidence by some and condemned by others.

It is two-directional and simple to make; a large pear-shaped carabiner helps to lessen rope twisting and knot jamming.

Pull-Downs

A pull-down consists of removing the climbing rope from an anchor after a rappel. In some circumstances, equipment may have to be left behind (e.g., descending ring, chain link, carabiner, sling).

The most basic pull-down (Figure 6–22) can be done when the rope is long enough to be doubled and can simply be looped around an anchor (e.g., a tree).

Figure 6–21 Munter Hitch **Figure 6–22 Double-line Flirt**
Right

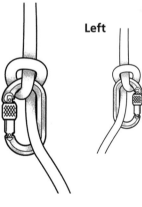

Left

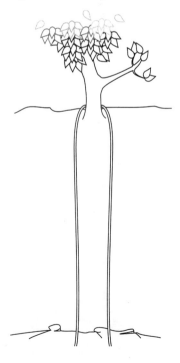

When a climber is solo, after the double-line rappel, the rope is first flirted, then one strand is pulled until gravity brings down the rest. When there are several who are going to rappel, the first rappeller can descend on a single, anchored half of the line and then anchor the line at the bottom of the rappel; the other rappellers can then descend on a single line. Or everybody can double-line rappel (not recommended).

When there is a possibility of rope abrasion, use a sacrificial sling and descending ring or carabiner to place the pull-down away from the rough or cutting anchor (always use a metal ring or 'biner in the assembly when using kermantle or webbing, as nylon rubbing on nylon will severely damage the sling).

On a short drop or when abrasion won't be a problem (e.g., with manila rope, etc.), one can use the Steeplejack's One-Hitch (Figure 6–24):

A retrieval cord may be used in several pull-down rigs.

Figure 6–23 Sling and Ring   **Figure 6–24 Steeplejack's One-Hitch**

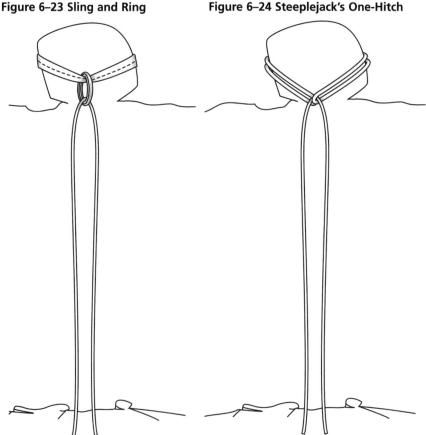

In an Eye Splice and Toggle pull-down (Figure 6–25), a loop is made in the end of the climbing rope and secured with a toggle and retrieval cord, as shown (no abrasion, no sacrificial equipment):

After the rappel, flirt the climbing rope and spill the toggle with the retrieval cord.

A Fifi Hook and retrieval cord (Figure 6–26) has been used on short-drop pull-downs (when the target zone ground is soft and the hook and 'biner won't bounce, ricochet and develop hairline fractures and have to be discarded).

The spill line is secured to the eye of the Fifi Hook. The assembly has a sacrificial sling and ring.

Figure 6–25 Eye Splice and Toggle   **Figure 6–26 Fifi Hook and Spill Line**

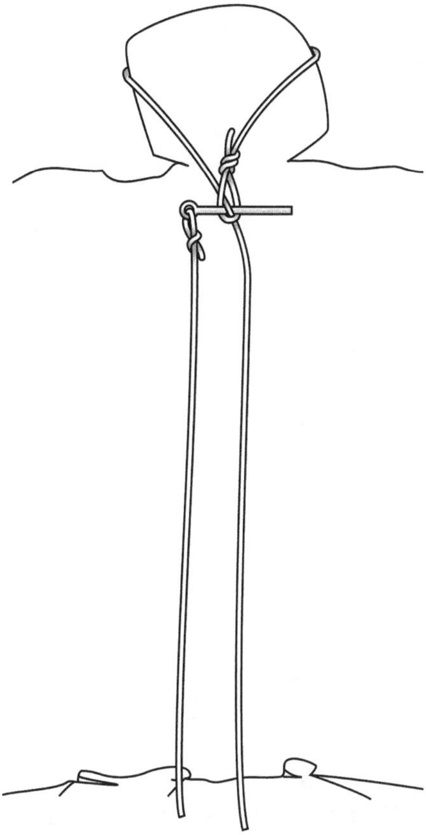

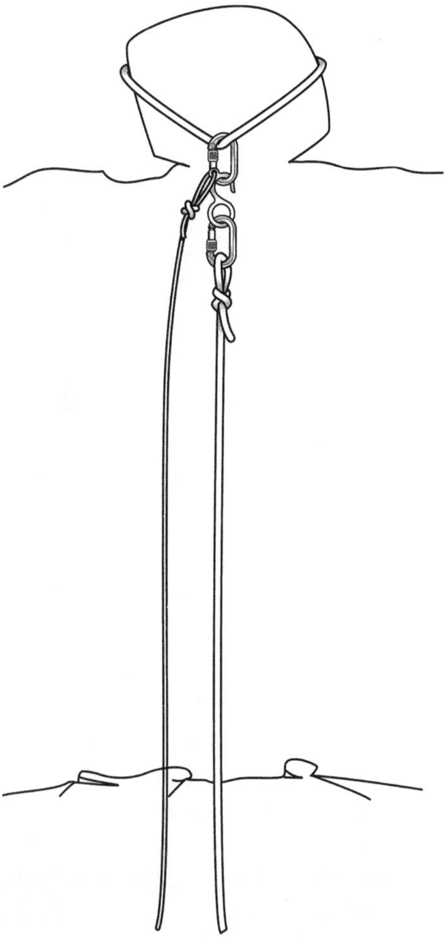

Another retrieval cord pull-down is (Figure 6–27):

Figure 6–27 Stopper and Spill Line Right

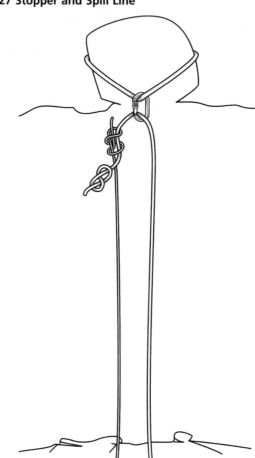

The assembly consists of a stopper knot in the end of the climbing rope (Figure Eight Knot or Stevedore's Knot), backed up by a One-Sided Grapevine Knot, also called a Half-Double Fisherman's Knot. A metal washer may also be needed as a stopper, depending on the size of the sacrificial chain link, descending ring or carabiner.

Over the years, several slip-type knots have been used as pull-downs, both in a doubled rope and with a single-line climbing rope secured to a retrieval cord. They are dangerous, not recommended, and are relegated to the realm of daredevils and derring-do stunt artists and circus performers.

7

Haul Systems

Introduction

Raising or lowering heavy gear requires a haul system. The simplest system consists of several people pulling on or holding onto a rope to which is attached the load to be raised or lowered. To minimize abrasion might require a pulley which is anchored and through which the rope passes.

Ropes and pulleys (blocks) are combined to serve as tackles, mechanical devices which transfer power for pulling, raising or lowering objects. When tackles are combined with poles and lashings, machines are the result.

A pulley normally has one or more wheels, called sheaves, which turn on an axle inside a case (a rope pulley is one which has no wheel; it's constructed with rope only and several examples will be given).

The mechanical advantage of a tackle (neglecting friction) is indicated by a number in the load symbol in the illustration. It's equal to the sum of ropes or cables which enter and exit the movable block.

A tackle can be used to pull on the hauling rope of another tackle (e.g., Whip-on-Whip, Luff-on-Luff, etc.); more power is gained but it takes more rope and time to move the load. If the load has to be moved farther than the longest rope can reach, the lift is divided into sections; climbers use a one-way cam device to hold the load while the tackle is reset.

Tackles

Single Whip (Figure 7–1)
The tackle changes the direction of the applied force but gives no mechanical advantage, i.e., the pull and lift are equal, minus friction (indicated by the figure 1 in the load symbol).

Runner (Figure 7–2)
The tackle is the inverse of the Single Whip. The lift is twice the pull.

Figure 7–1 Single Whip

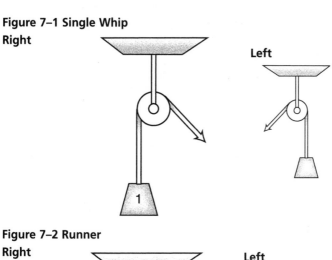

Figure 7–2 Runner

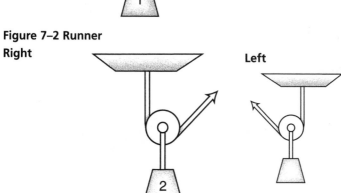

GUN TACKLE (Single Purchase) (Figure 7–3)

A purchase is a tackle that has pulleys which all contain the same number of wheels.

Figure 7–3 Gun Tackle

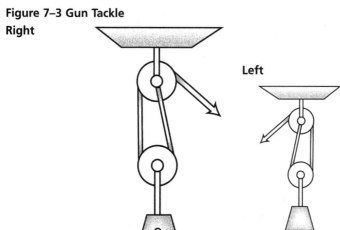

Inverted Gun Tackle (Figure 7–4)

Figure 7–4 Inverted Gun Tackle

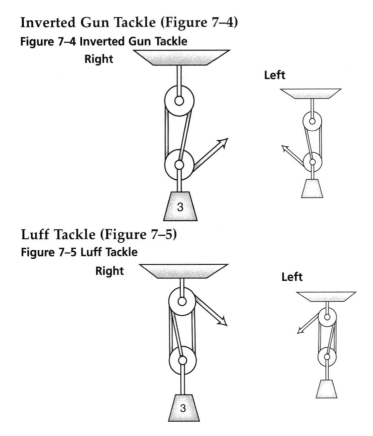

Luff Tackle (Figure 7–5)

Figure 7–5 Luff Tackle

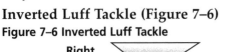

A small Luff Tackle with a rope tail on the stationary pulley is also called a Watch Tackle, a Handy Billy or a Tail Tackle; when there are two rope tails, it's also known as a Jigger or a Jig Tackle. The tail, or tails, are temporarily secured around a pole, another rope, etc., to provide quick, or additional, lifting power. It's used only for short lifts.

Inverted Luff Tackle (Figure 7–6)

Figure 7–6 Inverted Luff Tackle

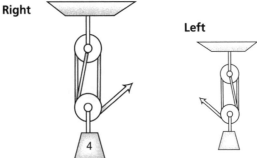

DOUBLE PURCHASE (Two-Fold Purchase) (Figure 7–7)

Figure 7–7 Double Purchase

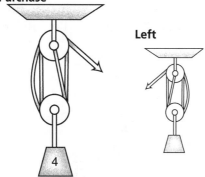

Inverted Double Purchase (Figure 7–8)

Figure 7–8 Inverted Double Purchase

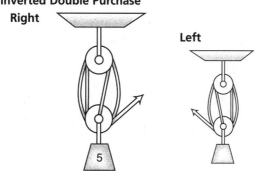

Whip-on-Whip (Figure 7–9)

Figure 7–9 Whip-on-Whip

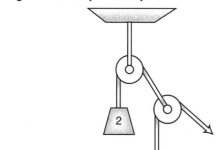

Double Whip (Figure 7–10)

The tackle is similar to the one above and has two uses. It can be used when a pulley may have an eye but no hook. It is also used when it is desired to distribute the load on the anchor, e.g., a pole.

Figure 7–10 Double Whip

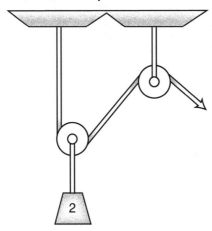

Piggyback Tackle (Figure 7–11)

The tackle is commonly used by climbers when raising a heavy load. The anchor may be distributed or divided as shown, or a single anchor (e.g., a tree) may be used.

Figure 7–11 Piggyback Tackle

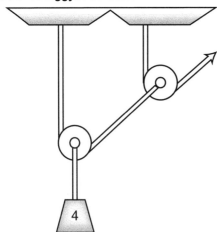

Z Rig (Figure 7–12)

The tackle is commonly used by climbers when raising a heavy load.

Figure 7–12 Z Rig

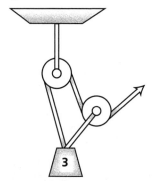

8-to-1 Tackle (Figure 7–13)

Figure 7–13 8-to-1 Tackle

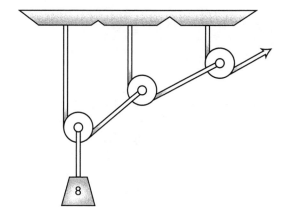

Rope Pulleys

The Pulley Knot (Figure 7–14), also known as a Trucker's Hitch or a Waggoner's Hitch, is used both as a rope pulley and to tightly lash down a load to a truck, wagon, etc. The pulling power is almost doubled.

Figure 7–14 Pulley Knot

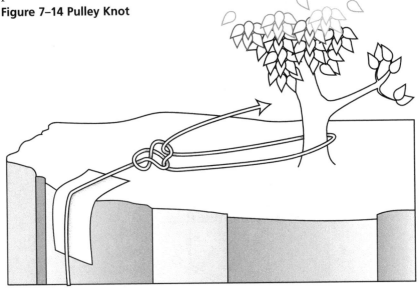

Other versions of the knot exist, for use in temporary or semi-permanent applications, in which the small loop above is replaced by a Half Hitch or a seizing. Other names for the different versions include the Truckman's Hitch and Drayman's Hitch.

There is also a more elaborate version which includes a Bowline, Two Half Hitches, various sliding loops, bights, etc.

The Lumberjack Pulley (Figure 7–15a) is a rope pulley and is used to move heavy objects.

Tie one end of the rope to the load. Make a small Overhand Loop in the rope, in the bight. Lead the rope around a secured post, nearby tree, etc., back through the loop and around the post again in the same direction as the first turn.

Figure 7–15a Lumberjack Pulley

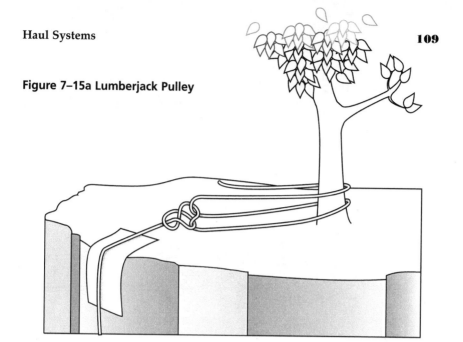

Make a second loop in the standing part (Figure 7–15b), near the first loop, lead the running end through it and back around the post again. Make a third loop and lead the running end through it and back around the post. Adjust and tighten.

Figure 7–15b

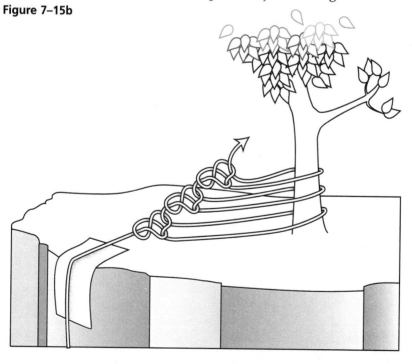

The Rope Burton (Figure 7–16) is used when the load is widely distributed. It is also used when it is desired to spread the pull, perhaps to minimize stress on an object being pulled or raised.

Figure 7–16 Rope Burton

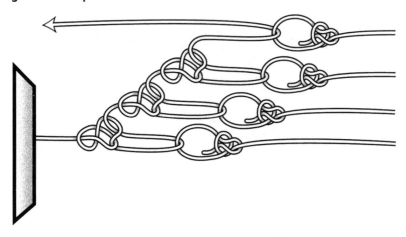

Figure 7–17 Poldo Tackle

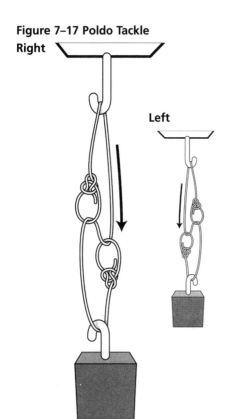

The Poldo Tackle (Figure 7–17) is used to hoist and lower loads a short distance.

Make a loop (e.g., a Bowline) in one end of the rope. Lead the running end of the rope through the loop and tie the end on itself with another loop.

Arrange the pulley so that the loops are close together. Pull on the rope (at the arrow in the illustration) to raise the load.

Base Camp Knots

Introduction
Coils and Chains
    U Coil
    Robbins Coil
    CAVER'S COIL (Mountain Coil)
    Backpacker's Coil
    Lapped Coil
    Rope Chain
General-Purpose Knots
    SQUARE KNOT (Reef Knot)
    Surgeon's Knot
    Marlinspike Hitch
    BARREL HITCH (Can Sling)
    MILLER'S KNOT (Bag Knot)
    Timber Hitch
    Sheepshank
    Lark's Head with Toggle
Tent Stake and Guy-Line Knots
    Tautline Hitch
    Adjustable Jam Hitch
    Guy-Line Hitch
    Adjustable Bend
Lashings
    Square Lashing
    Diagonal Lashing
    Shear Lashing
    Tripod Lashing
Backpacking Hitches
    Diamond Hitch
    Double Diamond Hitch
    Waggoner's Hitch (PULLEY KNOT,
      Trucker's Hitch)

Introduction

Many knots mentioned in previous chapters also have applications around the base camp, trailhead, etc., e.g., Bowline, Sheet Bend, Clove Hitch, etc., and won't be repeated here.

This chapter presents knots which complete the repertory of the knots normally needed and used around camp.

Coils and Chains

Another term for a climbing rope is a lifeline. Treat it as such.

When not in use, rope should be hung up to dry, coiled and then stored in a cool, dry place. A rope should also be coiled when transporting it.

Before coiling, let the rope hang free if possible and flirt it to remove all kinks and tangles.

If part of the rope is in use and secured at one end, begin the coil at the secured end, not at the free end.

A fairly simple climber's coil is the U coil, (Figure 8–1a) (only a couple of turns are shown, for clarity); to save arm strength, make the coil around the head and neck, over the shoulder and down to the waist:

Figure 8–1a U Coil

Right

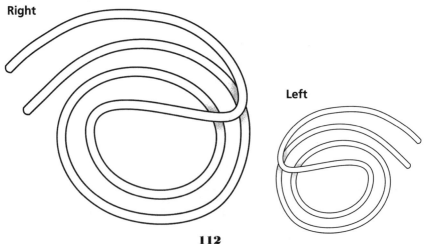

Left

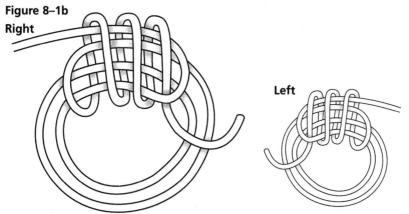

Figure 8–1b
Right

Left

Pull on the free ends to snug and dress the knot. Secure the free ends with a Square Knot.

The Robbins Coil (Figure 8–2). The finishing wrap should be made with about five feet of rope.

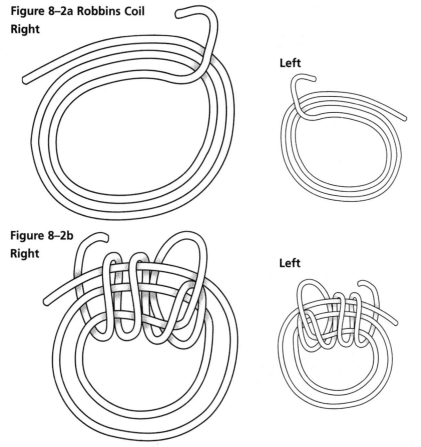

Figure 8–2a Robbins Coil
Right

Left

Figure 8–2b
Right

Left

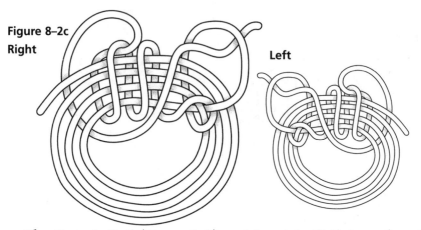

Figure 8–2c
Right   **Left**

The Caver's Coil (Figure 8–3), or Mountain Coil, is preferred by some climbers. A Square Knot is tied at the bottom of the coil before making the final wraps.

Figure 8–3a Caver's Coil
Right   **Left**

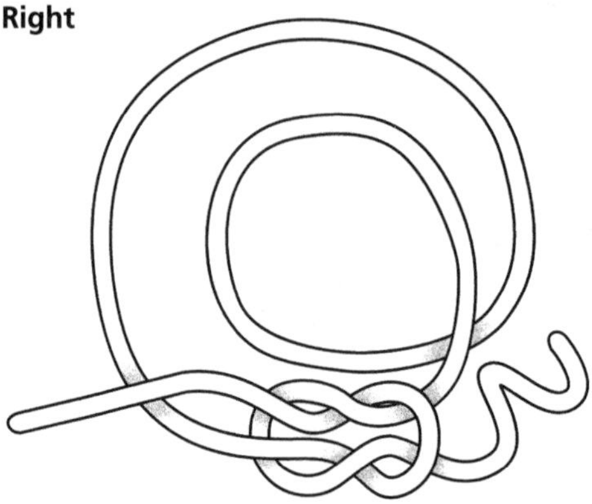

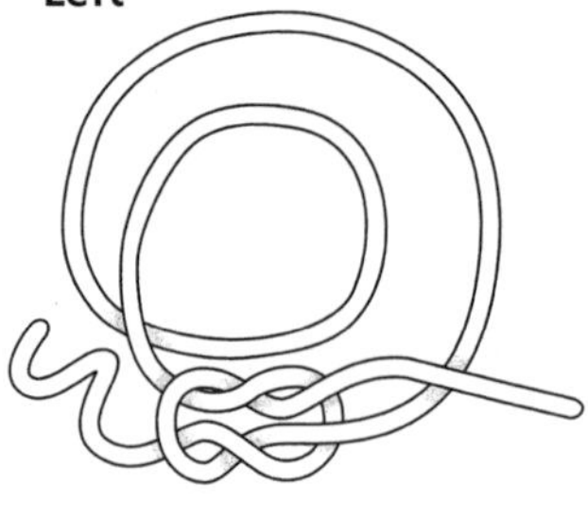

Figure 8–3b
Right   **Left**

Finish with a Square Knot at the top.

The Backpacker's Coil (Figure 8–4):

Figure 8–4a Backpacker's Coil

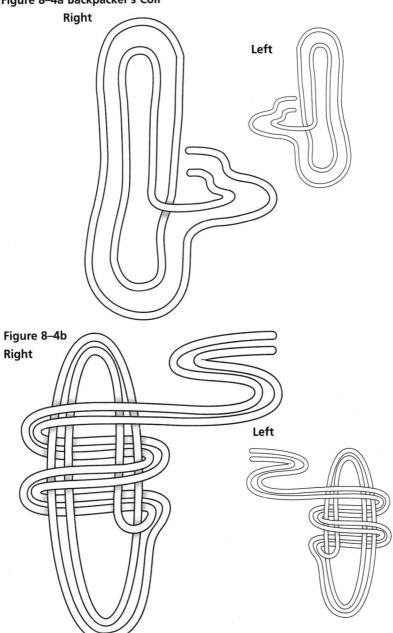

Pass a bight through the hank (Figure 8–4c) and lead the rope ends through the loop. Place the coil behind the back and lead the ends one each over both shoulders, around the waist and secure it in front.

Figure 8–4c

Right

Left

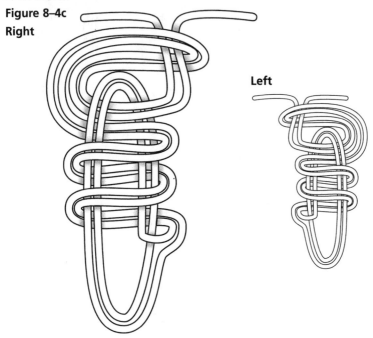

The Lapped Coil (Figure 8–5) is made with a doubled rope. Alternately lap the bights over the hand and then several turns around both sets of bights.

Figure 8–5 Lapped Coil

Right

Left

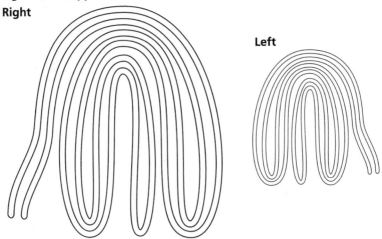

Figure 8–5b
Right

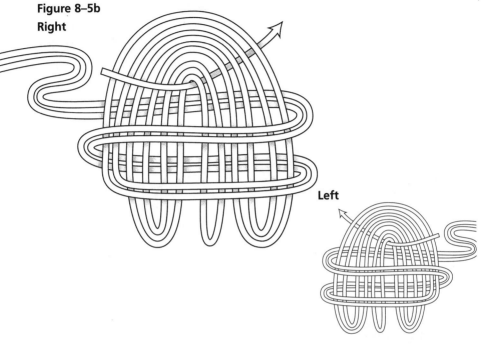

Left

Pass a bight through the hank (Figure 8–5c) and lead the rope ends through the loop. Place the coil behind the back and lead the ends one each over both shoulders, around the waist and secure it in front.

Figure 8–5c
Right

Left

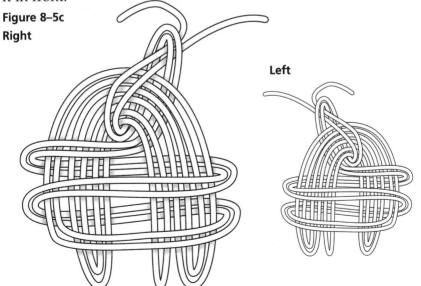

When the rope isn't too long (fifty to one hundred feet or so), some climbers prefer to make a Rope Chain (Figure 8–6). Double the rope and make the chain loops using a right-left-right sequence.

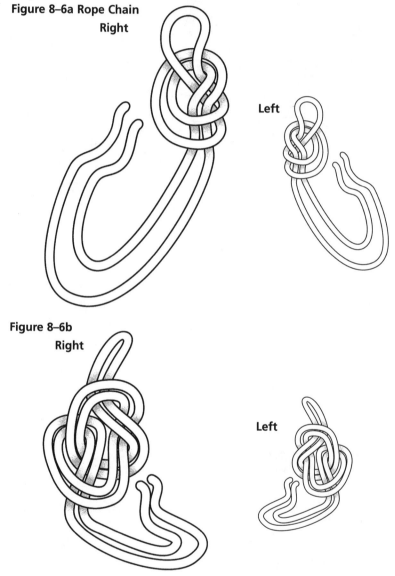

Figure 8–6a Rope Chain

Right

Left

Figure 8–6b

Right

Left

Figure 8–6c

Right

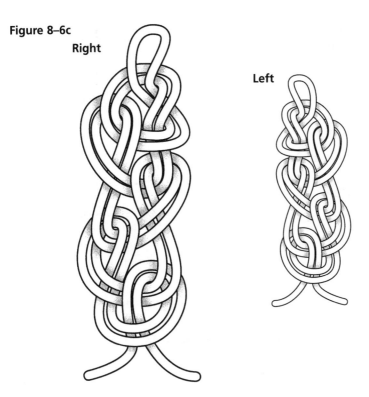

Left

Webbing may be also be chained, exactly as above. Dress each loop for compactness.

General-Purpose Knots

The Square Knot (Figure 8–7), also known as a Reef Knot, is used to join two ropes of the same size diameter. If properly dressed and tightened, it holds firmly and is easily untied. However, it can spill when the strain varies and is not satisfactory for use in climbing, rappelling, etc.

Figure 8–7 Square Knot

Right

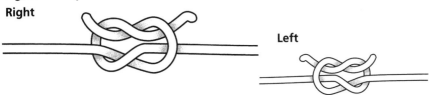

Left

Secure both free ends with an Overhand Knot or Two Half Hitches.

The Surgeon's Knot (Figure 8–8) is used in surgery, package tying and many other applications when it is required that a binding knot not slip while being tied.

The extra turn provides enough friction so that a second person isn't needed to hold the first half of the knot while the second part is being made.

Figure 8–8 Surgeon's Knot
Right

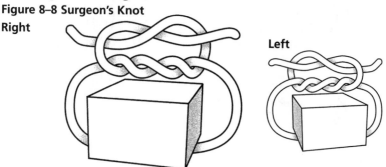

Left

The Marlinspike Hitch is used to increase one's pulling power when heaving a rope that may be slick, wet, etc.

Insert the spike, bolt, screwdriver, etc., as shown and tighten.

Figure 8–9 Marlinspike Hitch
Right

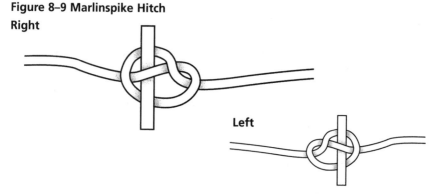

Left

The Barrel Hitch (Figure 8–10), also known as a Can Sling, is used when hoisting barrels and other similarly shaped objects. The connecting knot is a Bowline, but others will do.

Figure 8–10 Barrel Hitch

Right

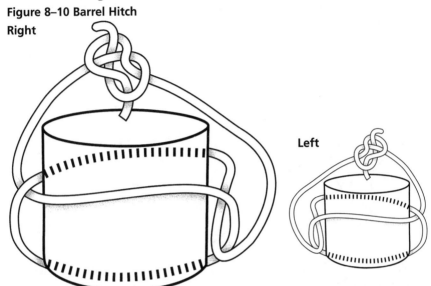

Left

When the hitch is to be used to hoist a metal cylinder or one which is slippery, two loops around the cylinder should be made (Figure 8–11).

Figure 8–11 Barrel Hitch with Two Loops

Right

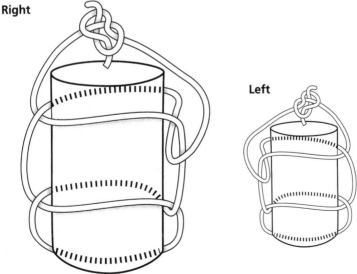

Left

The Miller's Knot (Figure 8–12), or Bag Knot, is a binding knot with many applications (e.g., it's used to tie sacks of grain or flour with heavy string or cord in a mill or on a farm).

It's similar to a Clove Hitch but snubbed more securely. Tighten and dress snugly.

Figure 8–12 Miller's Knot   **Left**
Right

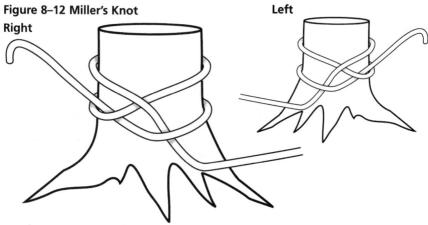

The Timber Hitch (Figure 8–13) is used when dragging a log or hitching a rope to a tree which will be under a constant pull. It can be tied quickly and doesn't jam.

If a log is to be towed, the drag can be minimized by tying the hitch in the middle and a Half Hitch at one end.

The hitch is also used when making Diagonal and Tripod Lashings.

Figure 8–13 Timber Hitch
Right

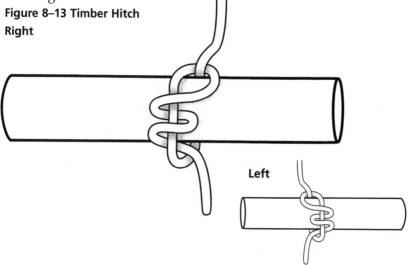

The Sheepshank (Figure 8–14) is used to temporarily shorten a rope or to bypass a section of damaged rope. The rope must be kept, as the knot will fail if the rope slackens.

Figure 8–14a Sheepshank
Right

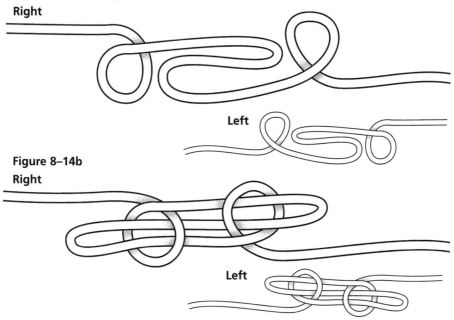

Left

Figure 8–14b
Right

Left

Figure 8–15 Lark's Head with Toggle

It can be made more secure by tying Two Half Hitches in each free end bight (around the standing parts) or by inserting a toggle in each end loop.

The Lark's Head with Toggle (Figure 8–15) is used to secure a rope bight or end loop to a ring or post. The knot can released by simply removing the toggle, carabiner, etc.

Tent Stake and Guy-Line Knots

The Tautline Hitch (Figure 8–16) forms a loop which will not slip when the rope is taut. It has great advantages for pitching tents; it can be easily tightened to stretch the tent cloth, it holds under strain and can be quickly loosened in case rain shrinks the canvas and lines.

Figure 8–16 Tautline Hitch

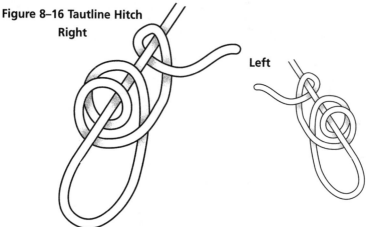

Right

Left

The Adjustable Jam Hitch (Figure 8–17) forms an adjustable loop which won't slip when the rope is taut.

Figure 8–17 Adjustable Jam Hitch

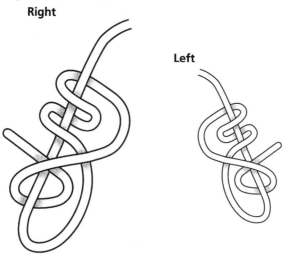

Right

Left

The Guy-Line Hitch (Figure 8–18) is used to secure and tighten tent guy ropes. It is adjustable and can be quickly loosened.

Figure 8–18 Guy-Line Hitch

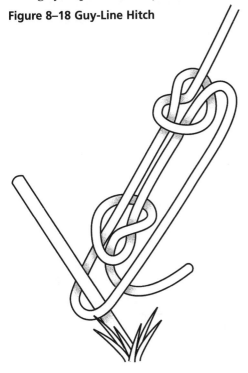

The Adjustable Bend (Figure 8–19) is used to secure a guy rope. It is adjustable and can be easily slid, even when the rope is under tension.

Figure 8–19 Adjustable Bend

Right

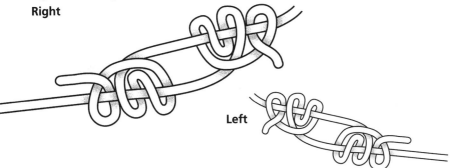

Left

Lashings

The Square Lashing (Figure 8–20) is used to bind together two poles which cross each other at an angle and touch one another where they cross (for poles which don't touch each other, see DiagonalLashing).

Tie a Clove Hitch around the vertical upright leg, just under the place where the horizontal crosspiece, or transom, is to be lashed. Then, keeping the rope taut, lay three or four wrapping turns around the leg and crosspiece, dressing as each turn is made.

Figure 8–20a Square Lashing
Right

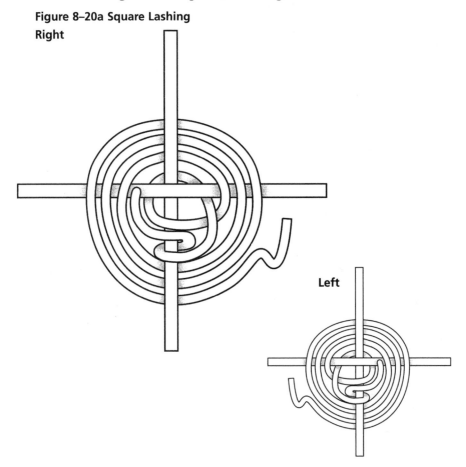

Left

Make two or three frapping, or crossing, turns (Figure 8–20b) between the poles to tighten the turns already made. Strain the turns and finish the lashing with a Clove Hitch around the end of the crosspiece.

Figure 8–20b
Right

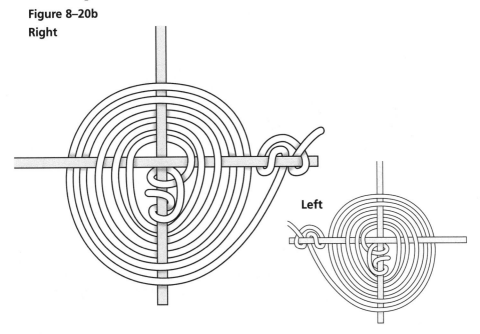

Left

The Diagonal Lashing (Figure 8–21) is used to spring two poles together, that is, to lash together two poles that don't touch where they cross.

Start the lashing with a Timber Hitch around the two poles at the point of crossing. Tighten it to draw the two close together. Make three or four vertical turns around both poles (only two shown, for clarity), laying the turns next to each other, not on top of one another.

Figure 8–21 Diagonal Lashing
Right

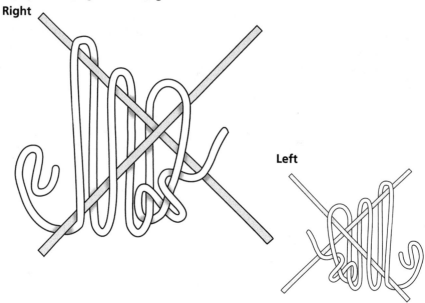

Left

Make three or four horizontal turns (Figure 8–21b), crossing over the previous turns, straining and dressing as each turn is made.

Figure 8–21b
Right

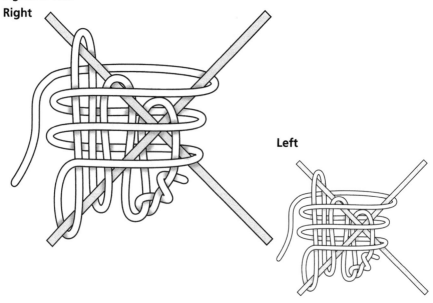

Left

Then make two frapping turns around the wrapping turns (Figure 8–21c), between the two poles, and finish with a Clove Hitch around either pole.

Figure 8–21c
Right

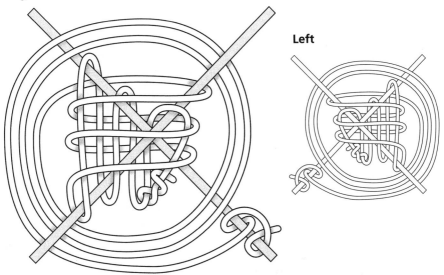

Left

The Shear Lashing (Figure 8–22) is used to bind together two shear legs.

Place the two poles alongside each other. Tie a Clove Hitch around one of them, at the determined distance from the top. Then lash both together with seven or eight round turns, laying the turns loosely beside each other.

Figure 8–22a Shear Lashing
Right

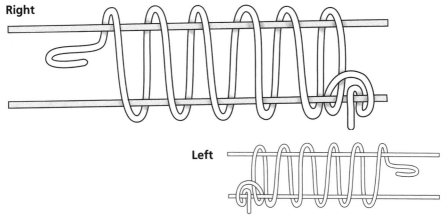

Left

Make two frapping turns between the poles (Figure 8–22b), then a Clove Hitch around the pole opposite the one on which the first hitch was tied. Dress the loose ends of both hitches. Open the shear legs.

Figure 8–22b

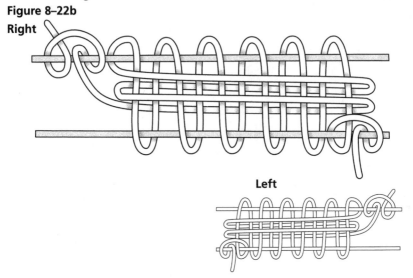

Right

Left

To make a more secure lashing, make figure eight, or racking, turns instead of round wrapping turns in the first stage.

Two Shear Lashings with tightly laid round turns and without frappings are used to lash two poles (overlapped) into one long one (e.g., to extend a flagpole); if necessary, put a long tapered wedge behind each lashing to help tighten it.

The Tripod Lashing (Figure 8–23) is similar to the Shear Lashing, using three poles instead of two.

Lay the poles on the ground so that they point in alternating directions. Begin the lashing with a Clove Hitch around one of the outside legs (some campers start the lashing with a Timber Hitch) and then lead several wrapping turns around all three poles.

Figure 8–23a Tripod Lashing
Right

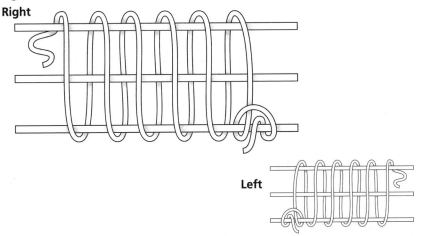

Left

Make two frapping turns in the two spaces between each outside pole and the center pole (Figure 8–23b). Finish with a Clove Hitch around the center pole.

Figure 8–23b
Right

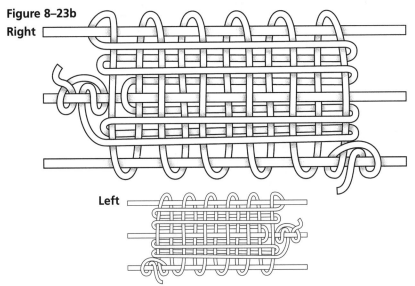

Left

Close the legs to assemble the tripod and dress the lashing.

Some campers prefer to start the lashing with all three poles parallel to each other and end-to-end. To assemble, expand the legs and dress the lashing.

Backpacking Hitches

The Diamond Hitch (Figure 8–24) is used to lash a hiking pack to a six-point frame. It's also been widely used to lash one or two packs to a mule, horse, etc.

It's begun in one of several ways, depending on the application. In the illustration below, it's begun by securing a loop (e.g., a Bowline) around the left point of the frame; other applications start with a Clove Hitch, leading the lashing rope through a cinch ring, etc.

Figure 8–24 Diamond Hitch

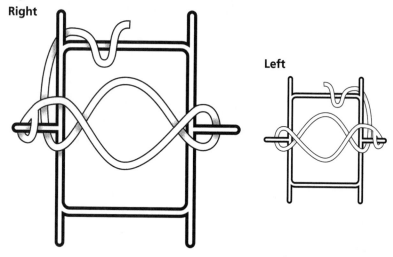

Continue as shown (Figure 8–24b), slipping two bights in the rope under the sides of the diamond and over the corner points. Tighten, dress and secure the free end at the starting point.

Figure 8–24b
Right

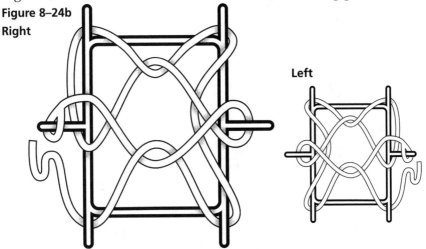

Left

The Double Diamond Hitch (Figure 8–25) is used to lash one or two hiking packs and a riding load (e.g., a keg, barrel, etc) to a six-point frame. It's also been widely used to lash a similar load to a mule, horse, etc.

It's begun in one of several ways, depending on the application. In the illustration, it's begun by securing a loop (e.g., a Bowline) around the left point of the frame; other applications start with a Clove Hitch, leading the lashing rope through a cinch ring, etc.

Figure 8–25a Double Diamond Hitch
Right

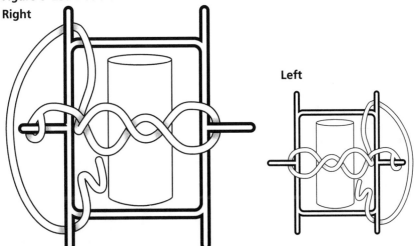

Left

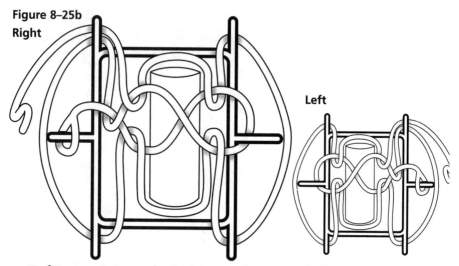

Figure 8–25b
Right

Left

Tighten and dress the lashing and secure the bottom and top of the riding load. Secure the free end at the starting point.

The Waggoner's Hitch (Figure 8–26), also known as Pulley Knot and Trucker's Hitch, is used to tightly lash down a load to a luggage rack, truck, wagon, etc. The pulling power is almost doubled when using the rope pulley.

Figure 8–26 Waggoner's Hitch
Right

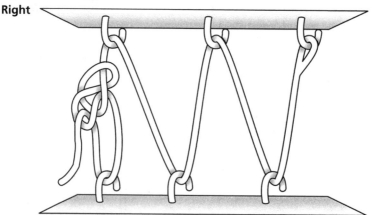

Pull on the free end until taut and **Left** then secure it by Two Half Hitches.

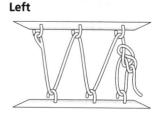

Other versions of the knot exist, for use in temporary or semi-permanent applications, in which the small loop above is replaced by a Half Hitch or a seizing. Other names for the different versions include the Truckman's Hitch and Drayman's Hitch.

There is also a more elaborate version which includes a Bowline, Two Half Hitches, various sliding loops, bights, etc.

Index